Naked in the Wind

Chemo, hairloss and deceit

S.A. Ledlie

 Some names and identifying details have been changed to protect the privacy of individuals.

ISBN-13: 978-1500136543

DEDICATION

To everyone struggling to cope with disfigurement

CONTENTS

INTRODUCTION

After deciding to bring forward our dream of moving to rural Brittany, France, we began searching for our new French home. Several months later we found ourselves preparing to leave our lives on the beautiful island of Jersey, Channel Islands.

Life at that time was carefree. Little did we know that 5 years later things would change so traumatically. It soon became apparent that I had become part of a 'dirty little secret' and a member of a club I did not want to join. It was a life time membership. Fragments of our lives as expats, living in France, are intermingled with my 'nightmare' that not only shook my world but left me unrecognisable.

CHAPTER 1
HAIR TODAY

How did it come to this, not quite believing I actually belong here, sat alongside all these patients. They all look sick! Each time the realisation hits me it's like being kicked in the stomach by a horse. Surely it has to be time to wake up from this nightmare.

As I looked around the clinic's waiting room it was impossible not to notice their tired, drawn empty faces. Were they thinking the same? Probably. It looked like we were all in the same boat.

There were a couple of male patients in wheelchairs hooked up to their drips, but mostly it was ladies looking as though they were recovering from the side-effects of chemo. Their hair was already growing back, all with a thick dark buzz cut look. My headscarf was still firmly in place. I assumed they had finished their treatment before me. I was so excited about my hair returning. *Hurry up hair, hurry up!* The novelty of looking like G. I. Jane had well and truly worn off.

What colour and texture would it be? I was a natural redhead, it was extremely thick and there was certainly enough to share between three people. As a child I would have loved to have been a brunette or blonde, anything but red! It wasn't easy to put up with the daily taunts of "been left out in the rain, Rusty?" and "carrot top." As a child you don't like to stand out in a crowd? Well, I didn't. I wanted to look like all the popular girls in the same year as me. During my late twenties my hair started to darken which was a welcome relief. Then, some years later, I decided to have some blonde highlights to help disguise the grey coming through turning it more into a strawberry blonde colour. *Yes, I love being blonde!*

My name is called out and I make my way towards Dr. Bernard's office. My oncologist had become a friend over the months of treatment. If it is possible to have a kind face then he has one. You can't help but feel totally at ease with this, seemingly, genuine man. He is a family man who loved to talk about his daughters and grandchildren. Someone who understood how it felt to endure this terrible treatment and I trusted him completely. It had been a lonely journey and it felt comforting to have someone that had all the answers and seemed to understand how it made me feel physiologically. You have to trust your medical team after all, don't you? He helped me enormously through my chemo sessions, squeezing my hand when I became tearful. Even getting me a private room so I didn't become even more stressed looking at other people having their drips fitted. He said all the right calming words (in perfect English too), I thought he was a wonderful, caring doctor; never tiring of my emails to him with my relentless questions. And they really were relentless!

"So, how are we feeling today?"

"Good, thank you! And excited that my hair has started to grow back" I beamed at him; whipping off my headscarf and leaning forward so he could see the four colourless hairs sticking out from one side of my shinny scalp. He just smiled, flatly, and changed the subject back to the radiotherapy treatment that I was half way through. Everything seemed to be progressing well.

I continued with the radiotherapy sessions, always aware and slightly confused as to why I seemed to be the only patient in the radiotherapy waiting room still wearing a scarf. Not everyone had a lot of hair but they definitely all had more than me. *How come there is nobody here at the same hair growth stage as me? Odd.*

Two weeks later it was time for my next appointment with Dr. Bernard. This time he seemed slightly concerned about my lack of hair re-growth. Trying to reassure him it really was starting to grow as there were now ten hairs (yes I had counted each and every one) randomly dotted over the, still, very shiny smooth scalp. Not sure who I was trying to convince.

Over the coming weeks I found myself becoming more and more interested, or was that obsessed, with everyone's hair. Not just in the clinic's waiting room but in the street, supermarkets just about everywhere. If I saw a woman with a hat on I would have to see if there was any hair poking out. If anyone had a headscarf on, I needed to discreetly look to see if there was hair tucked away under it or if, like me, she too had a smooth scalp. I didn't realise this at the time, but I suppose I was staring at them. If our eyes met I would always look away, embarrassed.

During my chemotherapy, because of the side-effects, I didn't really care if I caught people staring at me. In fact, I wanted them to feel sorry for me having to endure this rotten treatment, feeling, ever so slightly like a pink warrior! But now the treatment was over and I was feeling good I didn't want it anymore and thought it was extremely rude. If I caught anyone looking in my direction I would glare at them, lifting my eyebrows, as if to say.

"Yes...what are you looking at?" In French of course. More often than not they would carry on staring as though they thought I was also blind. Infuriating!

Three weeks later, it was my follow up appointment after finishing the radiotherapy. It was such a massive relief that all my treatment had finally finished apart from the next 5 years on hormone therapy pills.

Dr. Bernard examined me and we spoke about the effects the radiotherapy had had on my skin. It had a slight tanned appearance but there was no burning even though I am fair skinned. Then it was down to business, my hair.

"We are a little concerned about your lack of hair as we have never seen it growing back like this (slow and very sparse) before." *Oh God what the hell is wrong with it?* I assured him that there were more hairs sprouting and it was just taking longer than usual, trying to convince him or myself again. However, underneath my smile there was a very small black cloud lurking. The type of feeling that gives you this deep rooted fear of something foreboding. Something you will fight to keep hidden for fear of it becoming a reality. But at the same time you are not sure what it is. He didn't want me to see him again for a couple of months. Leaving the clinic felt confusing I suppose. On the one hand there was the free time gained from not having constant appointments but on the other was the impatient longing to return to having a full head of hair and the uneasy feeling that seemed to be following me around. The longing to go outside and feel the wind blowing through my tresses was overwhelming.

***

The family had decided half-way through my treatment that we would go on holiday when it was all finished. It was nice to have something to look forward to. So, we took the children, both teenagers, to Tenerife and we had a wonderful time. It felt great to be a stranger and funnily enough nobody stared at me with that pitying look. They were too busy enjoying their own holidays. Relaxing in the sunshine, lots of swimming and eating out in the warm evenings was blissful, as was being able to taste food again with my taste buds returned to full working order. The holiday was what we all needed: just what I needed to put the very scary lonely months of treatment behind me.

Arriving home from our carefree holiday was the beginning of my 'new' normal life. The Breton spring had arrived and it was good to be out in the garden, planting some vegetables and tending to the many plants and shrubs that surrounded the house. My husband, John, made me a little greenhouse so I could grow tomatoes and get other seeds started. It was easy to get lost in there for hours. I got a bit carried away and ended up growing enough tomatoes for the entire town. Life was different but good. Seeing the world in colour and 3D again was so uplifting. The first thing I remember, on being told my diagnosis, and walking out into the clinic's car-park noticing the trees and leaves in great detail and thinking I wouldn't see them for much longer. Even though my medical team had told me if I had all the treatment they were hopeful I would make a good recovery. The first time you hear the word 'cancer' instantaneously your world comes crashing down around you. You don't hear them telling you the good (if you are lucky enough) prognosis, you go deaf and think it is the end.

It was still early days after finishing my treatment for breast cancer and of course I still had worries, it was easy to panic about the slightest thing, but I just kept reminding myself it was normal to feel like this. Dr. Bernard had asked me on the last day of my treatment how I felt.

"Scared that I won't be coming in for treatment, feeling scared that I won't have you as my security blanket." He reassured me that all his patients told him the same. I am sure he must regret the very day he gave me his email address. He passed me my prescription to start taking my first pill that I would have to take every day for the next 5 years. Believe it or not it was worrying swallowing that first one. You imagine instant side effects. He told me to take it at bedtime with a glass of milk as I would be asleep during any side effects you might feel in the first few hours of taking it. Anyway, it was good to wake up the next morning! Then, of course, I forgot about the possible side effects and just popped it every night without a second thought. There were some aches and pains to contend with after a few weeks and the 'hunger', oh my god the hunger! The weight started to pile on. Each week the damn scales screaming at me,

"That's another half a kilo!" Being constantly hungry plus suddenly being able to eat massive portions was not like me at all. Every meal time I would hope that one of the children wouldn't be able to finish their food so I could eagerly grab their plates and polish off their leftovers! Several times, during each meal I would try to sound casual,

"Have you finished?" I reached my hand over in hopeful anticipation. Being bloated and very uncomfortable after each meal wasn't enough to put me off. Then there were the between meal snacks. Let's not forget the hot flushes, they were…HOT.

I would remove my headscarf when the school next door was closed as it became reasonably private. It made me feel naked to have nothing on my head and I always had to have a hat or scarf stuffed into a pocket just in case someone would suddenly appear at the gate. If the sun was out it would reflect off my scalp like the force of a halogen light. It was also impossible to be completely at ease even inside my own home. If I heard someone letting themselves in to the house I would panic shouting out,

"Who is it, are you on your own?"

It wasn't long before the kids used to automatically call out as soon as they were coming in that someone was with them or more often than not, they would send me an sms to tell me. Although very thoughtful of them, it also made me feel guilty at taking away their spontaneous life. It made me wonder if it was because they would be embarrassed in front of their friends to see their mum looking like a little old man, or because they knew I would be mortified. To think they might be embarrassed about how I looked was unbearable. They both said it was because they knew I would be embarrassed. Right answer!

***

My next oncologist's appointment soon came round. Of course this always meant the dreaded blood tests, praying the nurse would find a vein on the first go. Having arrived at the clinic clutching my blood results I was all hot and bothered, late, as usual.

After apologising to the receptionist and blaming the overflowing car park for my terrible time keeping, I was immediately called in to see Dr. Bernard. Sitting down in the now familiar chair - my chair - I removed my headscarf to show him the regrowth. My stomach was tensing in anticipation of his reaction. Some more hairs had appeared above my ears giving me a 'monks' appearance. It wasn't a great look. In fact it looked really, really ugly. It made me look like I should be on the film set of the latest Robin Hood film starring as Friar Tuck! He looked uncomfortable, but at the same time as though he was half expecting to see it. My black cloud increased in size, waiting.

"We have never come across this before, I am going to call the drug company." *Oh no, what is wrong with my stupid damn scalp! Please don't call them it will be fine.*

"Oh, okay if you think it is necessary," thinking he was being a bit hasty but...

A month later it was time to see my consultant, Dr. Laurent (thanfully she was fluent in English too) for my check-up. She was a very tall woman with short dark hair and an extremely deep voice.

I was not really sure she knew how to smile and she always seemed a bit hard, unsympathetic and emotionless but I suppose it was the nature of her job.

Whilst I was in the waiting room, thinking it should be my turn next, Dr. Bernard walked by and noticed me. Or had he come looking for me? Beckoning me over, we stood to one side of the corridor away from prying eyes and straining ears.

"I have spoken to the drug company (Sanofi Aventis); they informed me that you are only the 3rd or 4th person in the world that this has happened to. Your hair is not going to grow back, I am very sorry."

My name was called out to go into Dr. Laurent's office. The rest is a blur. Shock, horror, light-headed, numb, deafness shrouded me to anything the consultant had to say. All I could think about was those unbelievable words Dr. Bernard had just spoken to me. He didn't look ...well anything really. Shouldn't he look a little sorry? Why did he tell me in such a casual, nonchalant way? Trying to play it down? Perhaps he thought if he told me in his office I would have a meltdown: of course that would have happened for sure. Perhaps he didn't have time for my drama. After all, they had treated my cancer so that was their job done, but what about the collateral damage? Why did this happen? Why was hair growing everywhere else? What other permanent damage did this drug do?

Dr. Laurent showed me out of her office, I felt

sick and couldn't think straight. Standing at the reception and handing in my medical card I was on autopilot, now I had to find the medical taxi driver to take me home. He was enjoying a coffee and cigarette outside with the other taxi drivers who were also waiting for their patients. Normally I would have the same friendly driver and today was no different. Perhaps an unknown driver today would have been easier.

The forty-five minute journey seemed to take a lifetime. The sky was grey and the drizzle was quickly turning into heavy rain, resembling what was going on in my head. Rush hour traffic was bumper to bumper to get out of the city and as usual the friendly driver wanted to make small talk. It was impossible to speak to him, I didn't want to. Instead, I just stared out of the back passenger window and didn't care what he thought of my rudeness. My gaze fixed through a piece of steamed-up glass with beads of rain running down the outside.

Just shut up for god's sake! I wanted to scream at him, tell him to shut up and get me home. After what seemed a life time we pulled up outside home and walking through the front door I wept. They were big, fat, devastating tears of disbelief.

No, they had to be wrong. This can't be right, it can't be happening, this is unheard of. For the first time since being diagnosed with breast cancer thinking *why me, how could I be the third or fourth person in the world!? It just doesn't make any sense. How do they know? They're wrong. They HAD to be wrong.*

Over the coming days denial set in. I refused to believe it, they were definitely wrong it was going to grow back. There was no way my head was going to stay like this for ever, absolutely no way.

As the weeks passed there were a few more hairs appearing around my ears they were very dark and a strange texture; no sign of red at all. The more that grew the worse it looked! Deciding then that it looked much better to have none than this!

Of course Google became my new best friend.

I was filled with a glimmer of hope, some magic potion was out there and it will return my thick head of beautiful auburn hair. I did not really care if it grew back red, black or green. My search for the Holy Grail of hair restoration began.

Hour after hour was spent tapping away on the keyboard, trying to think of search terms that would come up with a solution: something that would give me a glimmer of encouragement. There were many promises by companies and people that were going to save me from this life of permanent baldness and ugliness starting at the age of forty seven. There were gallons of snake oil to choose from too. Something was going to work!

The list was endless. Here are just a few:

- Nano particle shampoo and tonic
- Caffeine shampoo
- Essential oil blends
- Food supplements
- Herbal and mineral supplements
- Massage

- Reiki
- Laser combs
- Hair transplant

I tried everything on this list apart from the laser comb and transplant. A hair transplant wasn't an option for me as it was necessary to have a good area to harvest the hair/ follicles from and there wasn't a patch on my still shiny scalp that was good enough. But after looking into what a transplant entailed I would never have gone for one: far too gruesome. There was some talk about stem cell therapy although it was early days but maybe, one day. They had done some stem cell treatment on mice and they had grown hairs but the individual hairs had grown in all different directions. Poor mice, I would have happily volunteered to step in for them. My head looked so bad it really could not look any worse. It resembled either a toilet brush or a baby Orangutan.

I was hoping with all my heart that it would grow back before stem cell therapy was readily available.

Someone I had recently met kindly offered to come round to the house to do some Reiki sessions on me. She believed it was going to help me and I was willing to try anything. She also wanted to do Feng Shui on our bedroom which I thought might be worth trying but when she said our television had to go... We always like to go to bed fairly early and watch some TV and since this problem started, I needed the television on until I was falling asleep even with the sleeping pills. It was now a necessity to use sleeping pills, nightly. Although I enjoyed these Reiki sessions they didn't have any effect. That was another possibility to cross off the list.

Each time I looked in the mirror there was a cancer patient staring back. It was as though it was tattooed onto my forehead. How on earth was I supposed to move on looking like this, it was impossible. By now, I was eating, breathing, living my hair problem. It had been all too easy to become obsessed; it was driving everyone nuts because it was all I would talk about. What else was there to speak about? *Why can't I just change the damn record!*

The black cloud was now increasing in size, bit by bit, every day. Often my head would feel like it was going to explode with all the negativity. Wasn't I supposed to be in the 'getting my life back' phase? Fat chance of that happening until this has been resolved.

Then something happened which changed everything. I decided to Google the name of my chemotherapy drug along with the words 'hair not returning'.

BINGO!

Right there, in front of me was another lady that had had the same drug combination as me and her hair hadn't returned either. Oh my! I could have wept with joy. In fact I think I did. It was like winning the lottery. She had posted a message on a breast cancer forum in America. My fingers couldn't type fast enough, creating an account and posting a reply to her. I wasn't alone anymore. If there were only three or four of us in the world then we must be two of them leaving another two out there. I kept looking for her reply but because of the time difference I had to wait till that evening. *Come on Pam, please contact me.*

***

Pam and I began searching for other women suffering the same disfiguring adverse side-effect.

Our support group was created.

It had only been a few days before another lady joined us. She didn't have any hair return not even lashes or brows. We were like the three bald musketeers. *I am not a freak!*

Our little group started growing with astonishing speed. This was REALLY odd as there was supposed to only be four of us at the most. Ladies joining us from countries that had recently started to use this combination of chemotherapy drugs including India, Germany but mostly America. The United Kingdom had just been given the go ahead to use it so we knew it wouldn't be long before some UK members would join us. It had been on the UK news that some patients had had to put up a fight to get this expensive drug as not all regions were able to prescribe it.

It seemed no one was being informed that permanent hair loss was a possibility before they started their treatment. Why were patients not being warned? It wasn't long before our suspicions were on high alert. We just wanted people to know about it and I would never advise anyone not to have this drug. It had to be their choice but it was their choice to make. Dr. Bernard telling me there were only three or four people in the world with this problem suddenly seemed a bit of a sick joke. Were they his words, his interpretation, or the words of the drug company?

We were all so happy and thankful to have found each other. We would spend hour after hour pouring our hearts out to, each of us with the same emotions and the most common feeling was that nobody was listening to us. It became crystal clear that we had become part of some dirty little secret. One that the medical world didn't want made public. *We would see about that!*

The weeks turned into months, our emailing list continued to grow. We tried to promote our support group, wanting to spread the word, through the breast cancer forums in the UK and USA. But we were met with a lot of hostility. Some of it quite vile. We weren't welcome, it's not what the other cancer patients wanted to hear, we were shouted down, there were arguments, swearing and so much anger. We were really not expecting this. What a shock. We thought our pink sisters would join in our crusade because this is what it had now become. It was our campaign to make sure all female patients knew about this around the world.

"Just be thankful you are alive," mostly got thrown our way. Of course it goes without saying we are all so thankful to be alive. There were a few that sympathised with us. We wanted to reach out to people with the same problem, make them realise they were not a freak of the medical world, which is what we had all been lead to believe. The burning question on all our lips was 'why were we not informed that it was a possibility' giving us the right to say 'yes I will take the chance' instead of denying us of our right to give informed consent. What happened to 'quality of life'? What happened to patient's rights? What had happened to Doctor's being obliged to report any side effects?

The battle had begun.

SUPPORT GROUP MEMBERS THOUGHTS

Anon

Unlike my breast, my hair is part of my identity who I am and how I see myself. We are identified by our head/face not so much by the rest of our bodies (we put a photo of our heads in our passport/driver's license etc.).
Moreover, the permanent loss of my hair was not part of the agreement when I started treatment for breast cancer. When I went for my surgery, I had agreed to the removal of my breast. When I started chemo I agreed to the temporary loss of my hair. It is cruelty not to have warned me of this risk when I was so vulnerable and could not look into the best options for my treatment.

CHAPTER 2
THE BIG MOVE
(BRITTANY, FRANCE 2000)

We had moved to the beautiful French countryside in February 2000. Deciding to take the big step, get out of the rat race and give the children the opportunity to grow up with a second language.

Our estate agent had taken us to see a lot of 'ruins' in North West Brittany because we liked the idea of buying something that needed some restoration work but the places we were shown were pretty hilarious! One was an old nightclub, close to Brest, in the middle of nowhere which didn't have any foundations in one room, just a massive hole where the floor should be. I threw a stone into the hole but didn't hear anything! The only good thing going for this disco was that just down the road was a canal. As John loves fishing this would have been perfect for him. I suppose taking us to the worst possible ruins he could find was a ploy. The last house he wanted us to see needed a mortgage, which wasn't the path we had wanted to take. We agreed to visit it as, we now realised, the money we would have spent doing any of these ruins up would have been far greater that the price of this house he really wanted us to see. So it did make a lot of sense.

We will never forget the first sight of Kerrougant. Slowly we drove down a very long drive way, covered both sides by trees and a large wooden farmhouse gate at the end, beckoning to us to come and let it cast its spell! Which is, of course, exactly what happened as soon as we walked through those gates.

Walking past barns, an entrance to a huge field, a large tree covered area and finally arriving at the front door, before turning round and seeing the most breathtaking views. The rolling hills and valleys of the beautiful Brittany countryside surrounded us. We knew we had arrived at our new home.

Grey skies and drizzle didn't stop us from running around the gardens and out into the fields, all of which was very overgrown. We explored the barns and discovered the back of the house had no windows and that it was called a 'Longere'. It was also 300 years old!

We wanted to sign for it there and then but of course we needed to sleep on it and let the estate agent know the following day what our decision was.

We dragged ourselves away from our 'home-to - be' and headed back to the hotel which was about an hour's drive away: getting changed out of our wet clothes and driving the short distance to the nearest town. There were a couple of bars, small supermarket and a Creperie. By now we were all starving so thought the Creperie would be perfect and we would get to sample a Breton 'Galette'. We looked at the menu, all in French, of course, and being clever I ordered something different from the kids and John. The waitress grinned at me.

"She is impressed with my French." I declared but the others were more skeptical. After several minutes of watching the cook creating the crepes in the open plan kitchen, the waitress brought three plates over. They looked delicious and smelt good.

"Oh no, why hasn't she done mine at the same time, I am starving?" They were all eagerly tucking into their mouthwatering meal as I just sat there. We could see the cook starting to make mine, and then the smell of something...putrid wafted over. The waitress kept looking over and grinning at me and then speaking to some of the locals and they were all sniggering. At my expense no doubt! The smell was making us all heave but John thought it was so hilarious that he was taunting me with every mouthful he ate. Then it was placed in front of me. It took all my strength not to vomit, instantly, over the plate. Of course, I couldn't eat any of it, so i just cut it up and shuffled it around the plate. Some of it was shared out onto the other three empty plates too. She came over to see if we wanted dessert. Having learnt my lesson the kids and myself ordered chocolate and banana while John had a citrus one. All four plates were sent back empty. As we were leaving the cook called me over and asked if I had enjoyed my galette.

"There was something on it, something coiled," I demonstrated by drawing in the air, as you do, "I didn't like that, what was it?" She gave out this huge belly laugh.

"Andouillette!" still none the wiser she pointed to her intestines and then said pork.

We all collapsed into our beds, exhausted from the day's events and excitement but there was not much sleeping done. We talked most of the night about the dream house we had just found and the massive decision we were making.

****

One wet and windy day,about a month later, we finished packing our two hired vans, including one cat and our precious little Jack Russell, Alice. We locked up our rented house in Jersey in the Channel Islands and headed off to the harbour to catch the ferry to St Malo, France. It had been a struggle painting the whole interior of the house back to its original beige colour, getting the garden tidied and all of our life possessions packed while working full time. Getting paperwork sorted was the most stressful for me as I am rubbish at it! As well as getting all the animals micro chipped and vaccinated for everything, selling our little beach business, finishing my college work and closing my pet business down. Not to mention two weeks before we were due to leave discovering our passports were about to run out a month later! There was the kids' school paperwork to sort out plus selling my car. But we managed it – just - and eventually we were on our way. We waved our goodbyes to Jersey as it disappeared into the horizon and started on the journey to our new life in France!

It was a rough crossing and as none of us have good sea-legs it wasn't too enjoyable. The kids were wandering about watching the front of the boat disappearing then reappearing, skyward bound, as though it was heading into orbit. John and I tried to lay flat and sleep to help stop us bringing up our breakfast. Both of us were dreading the staff announcement informing drivers to make their way down to the bottom deck to sit in their vehicles. However, as we clung on to the hand rails of the stairs, we made our way down to where the vans had been strapped into their parking space; it was a relief to see that both the cat and Alice had coped well with the rough crossing. There was a poo in the cat travel box but thankfully the cat was in John and Nick's van. The boat staff indicated to us to slowly drive off, with the French customs waving us over to them. John opened his window and the stench of cat pooh wafting through must have done the trick because they shrugged and waved us on: we were on our way!

When we arrived at Kerrougant the rain was torrential, but we didn't care as we excitedly lit our wood burning heater for the first time. The previous owners had left us some logs. We all got drenched taking in just the bare essentials. In fact it rained every day till June!

John had arranged to have a couple of weeks off work before having to return to his job in Germany so we tried to get as much done as possible. I didn't have a car so we managed to pick up a little mustard yellow VW camper van which I loved but the kids were embarrassed at the thought of turning up to their new school in it.

After a couple of week's holiday, Mellissa and Nick started their new school. I couldn't help but worry as I dropped them off on their first morning in the yellow camper. There were only three other English children in the school so they were a bit of a novelty.

We all settled in and I was meeting new people and was introduced to Sue, who would become one of my very best friends.

We decided to renovate one of the barns and turn it into a 'Gite' which is a little cottage. We were hoping to be able to rent this out to tourists in the summer months. After getting through the minefield of planning permission and red tape, work started.

When the Gite was almost completed, about ten months later, we needed some ground work to be done round the back of the house: guests would need car parking and space for them without them needing to use our private garden at the back. So the machines rolled in and cleared a large area of bramble and some small trees that were growing from fallen nuts. A large terrace for the Gite and an entrance into the field at the side with a play area for the kiddies was created complete with beautiful panoramic views. Perfect. Now, we needed to think about advertising. So much time and effort went into it and we were rewarded by plenty of bookings not only for the next summer but many weeks during the winter too. There was a property boom with lots of British visitors coming over to look for houses and barns to renovate. We were inundated with enquiries from house-hunters and tourists wanting bed & breakfast so we decided to renovate a large section of the main house into a B&B with 2 double bedrooms en-suite plus a large lounge downstairs. It took about another ten months to complete the B&B and we had bookings for it starting the day after we had finished decorating. In fact we were frantically still painting the night before our first visitors! It was around this time I started writing a weekly column for a UK magazine! There was no time to get bored.

The Bed and Breakfast was a great success too, providing meals for the weary house hunters I was often up till midnight clearing up and getting everything ready for their breakfasts a few hours later. Mellissa often helped me as we didn't have a dishwasher at the time and our kitchen would look like a bomb had hit it. She enjoyed it really; she says.

I would have to admit it was very hard work but enjoyable and would get a real buzz when I had repeat bookings. I became friends with many people that had started their French dream by staying with us on their first trip over: their last booking with us being the one which they signed the final papers. I shared many a celebratory drink with them. One couple came over on a tandem bike in search of a bar. They found just what they wanted, nearby. It is still going strong over ten years later.

We had an enquiry from a UK television station; they were going to start filming a family moving over to our little market town and needed somewhere to stay each time they were going to be coming over. They made the reservation and this included bringing with them a well-known British television presenter. The day they arrived with all their filming equipment was exciting, and with the amount of equipment it was good we had such a large dining room for them to store it. They had booked all of the rooms so it was no problem.

When we (well, the men) were clearing the ground round the back of the house to make a car park, we discovered a lot of wall ruins and on some investigation it turned out that the house we bought was in fact an old village!

We made friends with our farming neighbours down the bottom of our hill and with a British couple down the road on the other side. Judy and Pete would become life-long friends.

We felt we had settled in to our new French life.

CHAPTER 3
LET THE BATTLE COMMENCE

As each new member joined our support group, everyone said the same. Their oncologists did not inform them about a possibility their hair wouldn't return and all the oncologists' said that they had never seen it before. We even had two members from the same oncologist that told them both the same! How bloody outrageous.

I started researching and collecting data. It became the support group's mantra, research, research and more research. This uncovered some misleading information. A lot of brick walls were crashed into. All leading to huge amounts of frustrations and it was easy for tempers to flare. There were occasional arguments between the support group members.

It was difficult to sleep, when sleep would finally descend on me, I would dream that my hair had grown back and I would be touching it, it felt so good. For those few fleeting moments I experienced what it would be like until I would wake up and dash to the mirror.

Feeling so full of anger, I needed answers and nothing was going to stop me. Whilst it's normal for me to be hasty at times, when I commit to something, anything, it's all or nothing. Occasionally, though, I hadn't thought things through properly before acting on my impulse. This lead to the need for some damage control. On the other hand you can 'over think' things taking a lot of the fun out of your life. Spontaneity had been a big part of our lives, now everything had to be planned and carefully thought through.

By this time my family and friends were fed up with hearing about the 'ongoing saga' but it was impossible to let it go, I was just starting to uncover all the deceit and I needed to see it through.

Every time I found something interesting I would email my oncologist excitedly telling him the latest revelation. I knew he was just putting up with me but it felt good to have him listen. It was important to keep it fresh in his mind just in case he came across something that might be important for our case. However, there was always this nagging feeling that something wasn't quite right, that there was something I was missing. It seemed that both Dr. Bernard and Dr. Laurent weren't interested in what had happened, not bringing the subject up anymore until I ranted about it. There was just a gut feeling. *What was it?*

Was he always so patient with his patients? Or was he just making up for the lack of compassion shown by the consultant? Maybe that's how they worked together. In fact, as soon as I started moaning and crying about it, I was sure her facial expression changed from one of normal nothingness, to being slightly fidgety. She gave me the feeling she couldn't care less about my hair. On the whole I'd always try to find excuses for their lack of compassion about my collateral damage.

***

I was beginning to learn a little about the pharmaceutical world, other countries medical regulations, clinical studies and data collection.

After trying different search terms on the internet to find any new information, I came across a cancer doctor in Spain who had known about this problem for years! I couldn't believe it, so if he knew about it, why didn't the drug company and all oncologists know? They had to have known surely? *What the hell was going on?*

We began exchanging emails and he gave me a lot of very interesting information. This included the refusal of a well-known medical journal to publish his study in 2009 which showed that he had monitored 50 patients with severe long term alopecia after taking this drug and that none of the 50 had hair grow back up to and after 7 years. SEVEN YEARS! So it had been known about for years!

I wrote to Sanofi Aventis (drug company) and received a reply saying that they knew about me, from Dr. Barnard, and that it was very, very rare for this to happen and no, they would not be compensating me. I continued to write and email them which mostly went unanswered. However, one letter from them informed me that they knew that this adverse side effect happend in 3% of patients. I requested the data that had brought them to this conclusion. They gave me a chart marked with A, B and C.

Group A - Doxorubicin **without** taxane (Taxotere® is a taxane)

Group B - Doxorubicin **with** Paclitaxel

Group C – Doxorubicin **with** Taxotere®

Of the 496 patients assessed, 7 had prolonged significant alopecia (PSA) at a median of five years follow up. **All of these patients were in group C**.

The last letter said they couldn't help me anymore. I assume this meant don't bother contacting us again because you won't get a reply. I didn't believe, for one minute, that it was 3% and neither did the Spanish doctor. Neither did the person I contacted at a Swedish medical device company that was working on a new type of cold cap you wear during chemotherapy, to reduce the risk of temporary hairloss. She said she had no idea where the Sanofi Aventis got their 3% from.

Maths was never my strong point but one of our group members read the chart and suddenly declared:

"That's how they get their 3%! They added the patients that didn't receive our drug together, so that's all of them in group A&B and combine them with our group, C, and that's how they got 3%. When in reality, out of the 112 patients in group C that had our drug 7 of them had persistent alopecia. Making it now 6.3% instead of the inaccurate figure of 3%. No patient in group A and B suffered this side effect."

It was around this time that the Sanofi Aventis decided to change the wording on their website for this drug's adverse side effects to 'very rarely hair does not grow back' from 'hair always grows back'.

To say I was furious about the deception around the 3% statistic was an understatement! Big mistake!

It wasn't all negative doom and gloom. One afternoon I decided that a laugh was desperately needed but with the drug company in the firing line.

I am not technical, at all, so needed Mellissa's help. I wrote a little ditty. It was amusing and involved me making fun of my bald head until the end when inviting the drug company to (yes I am afraid to say) 'kiss my butt' and I mooned at the video camera. We had to do plenty of takes because we just couldn't stop laughing. It was posted on 'You Tube' of course. I thought it was hysterical, my family thought I had finally gone completely crazy.

Of course, I couldn't just leave it there, oh no. I emailed the person at the Sanofi Aventis office who had previously been in contact with me and attached a link to my video. Laughing all afternoon it felt good. It may sound rather silly and childish but what the heck. I have since deleted it but it was on for a few years.

We were starting to make ripples in the medical social media world but I wanted to go for tidal waves.

The frustration of nobody understanding or 'getting our message' was making me rebellious. It was obvious to me that being sensible was getting us nowhere. The drug company's refusal to help plus their misleading chart made them my no. 1 target, needing someone to blame, after all, it was their drug so it was their responsibility. The world of 'Big Pharma' was still very new to me.

I would think of something else, I had to make them listen to me, to us; they had to be made to admit the true extent of the problem this drug (when combined with other drugs) was causing to unsuspecting patients. It just felt so wrong, criminal in fact, to be dishing this stuff out to women that were already terrified and not giving them this vital bit of information. Let's be honest, any drug company will do whatever they have to do to protect their finances so they wouldn't want to risk women refusing their drug over something as 'unimportant' as their hair!

***

Several weeks later I was going to see my favorite rock band, 30 Seconds to Mars. Excited wasn't the word! As I looked up the street map for the venue I noticed it was close to a street name that seemed to ring a bell. Not being able to think why it seemed familiar, I shrugged it off. The next day, while gazing at the last letter Sanofi Aventis had sent me, there on the top of the page was the same street name. It was the drug company HQ no less!

A plan was born.

The day of the concert had arrived, I was so nervous. I headed off for the 6 hour trip, I was armed with my can of bright orange spray paint on the seat behind me. Even at this point I wasn't sure that I would actually go through with my hair-brained idea.

The brilliant 30 Seconds to Mars concert had finished, and still full of adrenalin, especially after meeting Jared Leto (the lead singer and Hollywood actor), I drove round to the back of the drug company's building and parked up. My heart was thumping. There was no one in sight.

As it was past midnight and not a residential area I was hoping there wouldn't be anyone else around. Walking along the back of the building, past the towering walls of mirrored glass, sirens wailing in the distance all added to this eerie scenario. Turning the corner I quickened my pace and carried on heading up to the front of the building, can of paint under my jacket. There were a couple of women heading in my direction but not wanting to hang around I just got on with the job as quickly as possible, keeping one eye on the 2 women (who didn't seem to notice me), but mostly on the main doors. Running back to my car as soon as the job was done and having to fumble with the ignition keys because of my trembling hands. My heart by now felt as though it would explode! Oh my god what have I done. The GPS was on. It took me back around the corner so it was possible to admire my work. It looks shall we say ...informative! Then to my horror the traffic lights outside their main doors changed to red! The adrenalin was still pumping round my shaking body not really believing what I had just done. What the hell was I thinking of! Come on lights. Nobody came out and the long journey back home began.

Mission accomplished, feeling elated and very proud of myself, I couldn't wait to tell my comrades in the support group what I had done.

***

It had now been several months since all my treatment had finished. There were a few more hairs but now looking more and more like male pattern baldness it was so distressing. It was torture looking in mirrors as I couldn't bear to see the old sick man looking back at me. A little sick old man or alien it was difficult to decide which was more appropriate. It certainly wasn't me staring back. Still trying any new lotion or potion on the market believing I could see an improvement but after a few weeks realised I was just kidding myself.

I continued to bombard the drug company with questions even though I didn't get any replies; even creating new email addresses to contact them in case they were blocking my address. Some days closing the shutters on our office windows in case someone would take a pop at me from the road. Realising it wasn't rational thinking but at the same time telling myself 'you never know'.

***

My daughter thought (for some strange reason) it would be a good idea for me to see a counsellor. She phoned up to speak to someone at the Cancer League, explained my situation and made an appointment.

When we arrived we were shown into a small room which was full of make-up and beauty products. Odd! A lady wearing a Beauty therapist's uniform entered.

"When will you be finishing your chemotherapy?"

She explained she would give me a make-up lesson first then have a chat with a counsellor after.

"I don't need anyone to tell me how to apply make-up thank you, I am a beauty therapist myself." Sitting there with a chemo headscarf on looking sick, not a trace of make-up, no eyebrows, half a dozen blonde lashes on each lid and a humongous scowl on my face. John describes it as my 'Bull dog chewing a wasp' look. I appeared to be anything but a beauty therapist!

"This is how your appointment today works, first I advise you on your make-up, how to make the best of your looks" the best of my looks! How bloody hilarious.

"This make-up lesson is then followed by your appointment with the counsellor," by now I had lost the will to live so it was easier to just sit there and let her tell me how to suck eggs. When she finished she passed me the mirror. What the ...! Who was this clown? This bloody woman infuriated me so much I wanted to stab her in the eye with her stupid make-up brush. It was degrading to be treated like this, so patronising. They knew why I was there so why couldn't we just get on with it. Damn them all. As always, everything and everyone filled me with anger and frustration. Eventually, after my uninformative, uninspiring ridiculous joke of a make-up lesson we were called into the counsellor's office. I can't wait for this!

She was young, very young, and attractive: my first thought was she must be straight out of University. My second thought was: how the hell is she going to understand about my problem. How is she going to understand about how it feels to look like an ugly sick old man when somewhere inside (very deep inside) was the bubbly fun loving 49 year old. Nobody was going to understand me because they won't have come across this problem before would they because it's so very rare: apparently!

She spoke very fast and my daughter had to translate for me. By now I was just sitting there, with a very nonchalant look on my face, and feeling very sorry for myself. It was becoming increasingly easy to feel sorry for myself.

Poor little, ugly, bald, disfigured me. The detestable self-pitying and self-loathing was, by now, a daily occurrence. After explaining to her that I felt the drug company had hidden data, that they were misleading patients and disfiguring women all over the globe, she announced that my problem wasn't the fact I hardly had any hair but was because I was full of anger at the drug company. Stupid cow! She then announced that she couldn't help me "Au revoir."

SUPPORT GROUP MEMBERS THOUGHTS

Suzanne. Northern California, USA

I obediently went through all the treatments: surgery, chemotherapy, radiation, and hormone therapy. My prognosis was good because I did all that. I thought I was informed about all the risks associated with each treatment, but hey, come on - where is my once beautiful hair? Where are my eyelashes and eyebrows? What is this "stuff" I now have sparsely growing on my head? It's been over THREE YEARS! Now I'm told that permanent hair loss is a known side effect of my chemotherapy treatments and after this length of time, it's not all going to come back – ever. I will spend the rest of my life as a bald woman. How can that be? I did everything I was supposed to.

CHAPTER 4
A NEW ADDITION TO THE FAMILY
(BRITTANY, FRANCE 2001)

Life was so different in France to what we were used to and there was so much to learn. I had hundreds of lessons to try to learn the language but it wasn't easy and I struggled with it. I could just about get by but vowed to never stop trying.

The children were speaking it well by now. Our son struggled at first but we arranged private lessons in the evening for him and they helped enormously. We were so proud of them. Hearing your child speak another language is just amazing.

When they first started at the local school one of the teachers stopped at the house one night on her way home from work; she lived just a two minute drive away. She said she would love to stop by a few evenings a week and give them any help they needed with homework or with the language. She became part of the family, joining in with our evening meals around our large farmhouse table with the wood burner blazing away. She took us on day trips at the weekends to places of interest; even my parents got to know her when they came over for visits.

Towards the end of October, there seemed to be an abundance of Chrysanthemums in all the shops, in fact, everywhere you looked. The most beautiful colours were on display so I couldn't resist buying a large plant of bright purple ones for our friend the teacher. I took them round to her house and left them on her door step as she wasn't at home. It wasn't until the following week I discovered the Chrysanthemums were traditional for putting on the headstones in cemeteries for 'All Saints Day' on November 1st. She never came round to our home ever again.

***

My daughter became friends with an English girl at school, Emmeline, and she would sometimes sleep over. Her father, Brian, would stop for a coffee and chat when picking her up. He used to tell me about their life when they first moved over. They had been living in France for many years so it was interesting to hear about their family's tales. He used to breed donkeys and this is how I came to acquire my very large donkey.

They were downsizing so he was looking to rehome some of his donkeys. They looked so cute, with their lovely long eyelashes shrouded by a band of white plus what looked like neatly applied thick black eyeliner.

"I know you are fond of my donkeys, how would

you like to have one – a gift!

"Really! You want to give me a donkey?"

"You know I would love one but I will have to check with John first." I was so excited and of course John said

"Yes, go on then." Rolling his eyes.

In fact, not only was I getting my own 'Grande Noir de Beret' but was also going to be a foster mum to her mother who also happened to be pregnant! I forgot to mention that bit to John. The new owner couldn't collect the mother for a couple of months so it looked like we would have her here for the birth.

We put them in a section of one of the fields with a tree sheltered area. They loved it.

One of my best friends, Karen, came out for a holiday, so when she arrived I introduced her to the 'donk' and instantly decided to call her (donk) Karen! This was much to Karen's (friend) amusement!

The weather turned awful and there was no break from the cold, wind and rain. It was relentless. With the new arrival due at any time, we decided even though they are hardy animals we had to provide some shelter for mum. We, well I mean John and Nick, put up some tarpaulin in the tree covered area and hoped the wind wouldn't blow it down. They watched us, well them, putting it up and seemed to understand what it was for. As we walked back to the house we turned round to see them both sheltering underneath.

The next morning I walked down to the far end

of the garden to see if the tarpaulin had been blown away with the terrible wind during the night. I certainly didn't expect to see this darling little baby with a huge pudding bowl haircut looking at me! I couldn't believe my eyes! He was adorable. We just stood there staring at each other; he was the most gorgeous little thing. It was obviously his first sight of a human and he wasn't sure what to make of me. His skinny little wobbly legs with knobbly knees were barely holding him up.

A few minutes went by when mum came over; you could tell she was beaming as only a new mum can do. Then Karen trotted over to join us and stood next to her baby brother. Mum wasn't happy about it and tried to bite Karen, moving her away, making it perfectly clear she didn't want to share her affection now with her first born. Karen slowly walked away from us, head bowed. It was such a sad act to witness but we made sure Karen got lots of attention and hugs from us all. But nothing could possibly make up for the lack of motherly love.

I informed Brian that the baby had arrived. He came over to check everything and tethered mother to a tree so baby would stay next to 'mum' and wouldn't decide to wander off. It was left up to me to move her about regularly.

Late one afternoon, while my friend Karen was holidaying with me, we walked down the road to have a meal with our English friends (Judy & Pete). After a relaxing drink and chat we started the five minute walk back. The sun was out, for once, and there wasn't a breath of air – still and silent. As we reached the corner and now on the home straight we could hear a strange shuffling noise. It sounded as though it was coming from where the donkeys should be so we ran the rest of the way. We spotted 'Karen', who was stood still just looking at us, then we saw baby.

"Where's mum"?

"Where on earth has she gone?" we couldn't see her anywhere, as we ran down the driveway and into the field, there she was. Where she had been tethered to a tree she must have been having a roll in the soil and somehow got her leg wrapped up in the blue plastic tether and at the same time her leg was bent and trapped under a root of a tree that was sticking up above the ground. Her leg looked twisted and broken!

"Oh my god, what do we do," trying to keep as calm as possible, we decided to get the tether off first. That wasn't going to be easy as she was snorting wildly and her eyes were bulging in fear.

I ran to the house to fetch a large kitchen knife and when I got back my friend Karen was, very bravely, laying on the ground leaning against her and trying to talk soothingly to her. We will never forget the sight of her terrified eyes! The one free leg was kicking out so it was really difficult to get close enough to start cutting away at the tether. Between us we managed it but the leg was still stuck and very bent under the tree root. Karen (friend) got up and as she did the mum simply pulled her leg out from under the root and stood up! She stood there face to face with Karen (friend), her bellowing nostrils (donkeys) almost touching Karen's face and neither moving nor wanting to break this emotional moment of 'thank you', before she snorted loudly and galloped off around the field!

About three months later the new owner arrived to collect mother and baby. It was very difficult (heartbreaking actually) to watch Karen's little face as she watched her mum and brother being taken away. A few tears were shed.

CHAPTER 5
BITING THE BULLET

A weekend in Switzerland sounded tempting. John had a short work contract there so we booked my flight. Treating myself to a new weekend bag (just has to be done) it would be good to give John a break from travelling and a nice change of scenery for myself but I do hate flying. It was freezing in Brittany, and even colder in Switzerland so I put on my thickest winter coat and my winter white, cute wooly hat to travel in. It's amazing how your hair keeps your head, in fact all of you, warm and since losing mine it was necessary to wear a bed hat as the pillow always felt cold.

Arriving at Brest airport with not a lot of time to spare (maybe that stupid counsellor could have helped me, instead, with my time keeping issues) and having to rush to get checked-in then quickly up the escalator towards security, and I placed my hand luggage and coat on the x-ray conveyer belt. The large burly security man beckoned me to walk through the metal detector. Just as I was about to step through he put his hand up.

"Remove your hat please." *What!*

"Err I can't, it's impossible," looking round at the queue behind me and trying not to panic.

"You can't go through until you have taken it off."

"Please, it is a big problem for me I really can't take it off."

"If you don't remove it you can't come through." So, whispering to him in defeat,

"I can't take it off because I don't have any hair."

"Oh, I am very sorry Madame, that's okay please go through." Phew!

I was sitting on the plane waiting to take off and musing about what had just happened: was he sorry that I didn't have any hair or sorry because he had asked? It gave me a laugh anyhow. We had a lovely weekend in beautiful snowy Switzerland.

***

A few months later, after John's contract finished in Switzerland we decided to plan a holiday, neither of us like the cold and it had been a long winter so we needed to go somewhere warm; we picked Southern Morocco (Agadir) as our destination. The hotel was nice and the food was delicious. The weather and the beach were perfect. Even though it was only very early spring time the sea was warm and we had great fun jumping through the waves with the locals most days. One night we decided to try our luck at the casino next door. Instead of just walking through the reception, security called us over.

"Sorry but you can't come in here with your headscarf on." *Oh no here we go again.* So just to make things easy I said, "I am having chemotherapy so have no hair" (sometimes it is just too much trouble to explain).

"We are so sorry, please go through," upon entering the huge, half empty room and not seeing any Muslim women in headscarves I then understood. This was just proving my point that everything in your life has to be well thought out to avoid either embarrassing or difficult predicaments.

***

To stop all these 'incidents' I decided to buy my first wig.

I hadn't bothered getting one when I was having chemo because it was in the middle of winter and thinking it was only going to be temporary, I didn't think it was worth buying one.

It was easy just to shove a big woolly hat on each day and whip it off at the first sign of a hot flush. We had dogs, chickens, rabbits, guinea pigs and a large donkey by now so I was always nipping outside.

I had to phone to make an appointment for a wig fitting. When we arrived I was shown an assortment of wigs and didn't know if I wanted to go for something very different or one that was as close to my original hair as I could. When buying a wig it does give you the opportunity to be frivolous and have a hairstyle you would never dream of having otherwise. At first I tried a few completely different ones on, the first made me look like Morticia from the 'Addams Family', then a couple of blonde ones but they just didn't look right. I was beginning to think it had been a wasted journey and it would be easier to just shove a hat back on. She then brought out a box and before she even fully held the wig up we all said,

"Yes this is the one!" It was like putting my own hair back on. It felt wonderful walking out of the shop.

Putting the wig on and looking in the mirror I recognised the reflection; it was me, I loved it and couldn't wait to show it off. I felt attractive and feminine, something that I had missed so badly. I even felt sexy again!

Strutting my stuff up town the following morning, market day, my first stop was the post office. Standing in the queue I wondered if either of the counter staff would recognise me. As I waited patiently for my turn to be served it was tempting to shout,

"Look ladies it's me! Don't I look amazing and healthy?" I am sure they (as well as most other people) thought I was constantly on chemo. When the lady in front had finished and it was my turn, I beamed the biggest smile at her, she did a double take and gave me a wink, grin and nod as if to say "That's great!" Walking out of the post office with my head held high, I decided to pop into the local coffee shop to show the owner, Sylvia. After devouring my pain au chocolate and my soup bowl of hot chocolate I decided to make my way home. Walking outside the wind had picked up and I caught a glimpse of myself in Sylvia's window and realised the wind was blowing the hair off my face and you could very clearly see the wig line all the way around my forehead and the sides down to my ears. Oh no! It looked... WIGGY and I instantly felt very naked. Frozen to the spot, I didn't know how to get home. It meant walking through the busy market, everyone being able to see my hairy hat. Not being able to face it I decided to take the long way back instead. It had never crossed my mind that when wearing one you had to think about the weather and I was suddenly not so thrilled with my beautiful new look! My elation had been very short lived.

The woman I had bought the wig from had sold me a roll of tape to stick the wig to my scalp for extra security. After removing the tape, before getting into the shower, and covering my head in shampoo it made this horrible greasy sticky glue spread all over my entire head. It was extremely difficult to get that residue off. The tape went in the bin.

This was my discovery that it's not a case of just shoving a wig on your head and that's the problem solved. So on windy days I still had to wear a hat.

There were regular visits to see my GP to get

prescriptions for various blood tests and the conversation was always the same.

"Hello, how are you keeping Madame Ledlie?"

"I am good apart from my hair problem."

"I wish you would let me give you some anti-depressants."

"I am not depressed, I just want my hair back and can't imagine living the rest of my life looking like this,"at which point I would dramatically pull my hat off and burst into tears.

"It would help you feel better about it."

"But I don't want to feel better about it, I HATE it and I don't WANT to like it!" I have lost count of the times we had that same conversation. I must have sounded like a spoilt petulant child. *What is happening to me?*

Thinking back this was possibly a large part of my problem, I didn't want to like it so would push any help away. Maybe it was stubbornness. Was it a natural mourning process? How do people feel when they lose a limb? When they are fitted with prostheses do they automatically accept it or do they fight against it, resenting their new limb. It was impossible to change my mindset. It was just this constant battle that the drug company had denied me my 'patient rights' to give informed consent for my treatment. I had been wronged by them and now I was permanently disfigured.

SUPPORT GROUP MEMBERS THOUGHTS

Sylvia from Germany

Four years ago I had 6 rounds of this particular chemo drug and my hair has never properly regrown. My doctors did not tell me that the hair-loss could be permanent. I signed a side effect information sheet and the statement in this sheet is: "The hair will grow back after the chemo treatment" (without restriction of any kind). Because of the permanent hair-loss, the wrong medical informing prior to treatment and the dismissive attitude of my docs and the manufacturer of this drug afterward, I suffer from deep depression and panic attacks. I feel betrayed, sad, helpless, desperate and frustrated. After 4 years I still have problems to look in the mirror. I feel ashamed of my mirror image. I do not recognize myself and I have lost my identity and the trust in the medical profession.

CHAPTER 6
GONE FISHING
(BRITTANY, FRANCE 2001)

John has always dreamed of having his own lake full of carp, so he can sit there all day, rod in hand. With all the land we now had, it was easy for him to make his dream a reality. After speaking with Allan our neighbour, the farmer down the hill, Allan said his mother was a water diviner and he would send her up to advise us.

She came trotting up the hill. Even in her late 70's she still had bags of energy, and looked around for some trees for the right branch to use. She stopped talking for a couple of minutes (a miracle in itself) while she stripped the branches of any leaves and fondled them to make sure she was happy with her magic sticks. Then she began explaining (we knew the silence wouldn't last long) about the mystic talents she was born with. This was followed by walking round and round, diagonally and horizontally until no ground had been missed. We didn't want her to catch our knowing smirks at each other, as the stick took a sharp downward turn.

After marking out the shape of the lake John wanted, I insisted on a small island for the ducks. Of course. The whole marked area came to about eight hundred square meters.

"We can offer fishing holidays too."

"Yes darling, as long as I don't see any maggots in my fridge."

Right across the middle of where the lake was going to be was an animal track. We weren't one hundred percent sure but thought it could be badgers. It started from the other side of the tree lined border (belonging to the farmer), over the 'lake' then through the hedge and over the verge on the other side. After which was the road so I didn't know where it went from there.

We hired a digger and a dumper truck and decided to use the dug up earth to create high banks along the inside of the hedge. This would give us and the holidaying fishermen some privacy from the road running alongside. We didn't want any locals trying to help themselves to John's beloved carp either.

The equipment arrived and we set to work. The dumper truck was my job; it was incredibly bumpy and was necessary to wear a good bra ... plus a cushioned seat!

Day after day we carried on, enjoying the work but there was no sign of any water. Early one morning John went out before me to be confronted by a badger barking at him from inside the hedge!

Four days in and still no water! We carried on deeper and deeper.

"Shirley, quick, oh my god look WATER."

Charging over in my little dumper truck, and there it was! We were so elated (and relieved!) it felt like we had struck gold and we celebrated with a beer or two.

Our elation was, unfortunately, short lived. The following day we realised it was actually the water table we had reached. Not really sure what to do next we just carried on to finish what we had started, complete with my little island. Many times anyone driving past would stop and want to see what we were doing. The crazy English followed by the traditional Gallic shrug.

After we had finished, it took another week to realise it was never going to be a lake. I felt like throttling our water diviner. It ended up being a huge expense for nothing more than an enormous hole!

Over the following winter it did fill up, to the top in fact, so we waited with baited breath to see what would happen the following summer. In the spring we even saw fish in it! Assuming they were there care of the birds or maybe the neighbours felt sorry for us. By the summer the lake was empty. John's dream, as well as the water, had sunk.

During the summer we were full of guests; they were free to wander round the land, pick nuts or fruit and, if the children were well behaved, I would let them help me feed the hens. One of the mothers came round the back to speak to me.

"I was walking in the field over there (pointing

in the direction of the lake) and wondered what it was? Is it some kind of Quarry?"

CHAPTER 7
STEPPING UP THE ANTE

Frustration had turned into almost constant anger.

The odd time a support group member would say the slightest thing that could be misunderstood, caused a disagreement which resulted in a member leaving. Some didn't like my occasional spontaneous outbursts of colourful language. Sometimes I would feel resentful at the members that didn't come across as being very 'active'. It felt as though they seemed happy just to let a few do most of the work, however, I tried to keep telling myself it IS a support group. Of course we hated it when we fell out, usually over something trivial, some just found it too much to cope with added stress. We had enough as it was and it seemed to be a constant roller coaster of emotions from excitement (when we thought we had a breakthrough) to the depths of despair. We were from all walks of life, all facing this distressing disfigurement, all been lied to so it was inevitable that there would be disagreements. We were so passionate and putting our all into being heard.

New members were continuing to join, a few ladies would ask to join us temporarily so they could ask us for information and wanted to download our data. As they were starting the same chemo regime they were horrified to hear what we were saying, and more importantly, to read the data we had painstakingly collected. They would ask their oncologists who would tell them they had either never heard of it or they had nothing to worry about and their hair would grow back. Sometimes the oncologists would tell them (when questioned) they had never heard of it, then when confronted with our research, would say that they did know about it but it was so extremely rare they had nothing to fear!

Genuine new members to the group would all ask the same questions and it grew increasingly tiresome having to repeat the same answers over and over again. It was always the same pattern, after asking the same questions they would then start with suggestions, the exact things we had been working on for the last three years. It would have been easy to say "just read all the data we have collected" but some just wanted instant answers without doing any work. Had I joined the group at a later stage I would probably have been the same. This world of 'permanent disfigurement' was new to them after all.

I never suggested to anyone not to have this drug but just to have the facts. Not to be lied to. We would tell them how we felt, the impact it had

had on our lives and to make their own minds up. Fighting cancer is lonely, your own personal battle. It was their life, their treatment and, at the end of the day their choice. A choice we had all been denied. They all seemed to appreciate our honesty.

It was around this time I received an email from a beautiful young woman, Amelia from the UK, she wanted to know the facts; she was a nurse and had been told she would face the same combination of drugs. We spent a long time chatting on the phone before her next appointment. After explaining about our group, and the research, I told her to think about it and not make any rushed decisions.

"Let me know what you decide Amelia and what your doctor says." She had her appointment, telling her oncologist she didn't want Taxotere® (and explained why) but could she have Pacitaxel instead (which has a much reduced incidence of hair problems). She was denied this option so opted, instead, for six rounds of F.E.C (Flourouracil Epirubicin Cyclophosphamide).

On my next check-up I asked Dr. Bernard if he could send me to see a dermatologist, seeing as my medical treatment had caused this problem. Because it is private here in France it would mean us having to pay for it all ourselves, it would be very expensive and why should we have to pay? He suggested that I contact a medical body here in France that deals with medical claims for compensation. He thought I should be compensated for my 'collateral damage' caused by my treatment. As far as I knew it was funded by the government, I have no idea if Dr. Bernard knew anything about how they operate. I can only assume he didn't or he might not have suggested it! He wrote down the name of this 'Committee'. Before leaving his office he had something else to tell me.

"We have decided to start a study (in the North West of France) to see how widespread this problem is as we are getting concerned about the frequency of occurrences."

"Oh! That's great news." This was an exciting and an unexpected move in the right direction. At last some action.

"There are around fifteen other clinics and hospitals in this region taking part in it."

"How long will this study last?"

"I have no other knowledge about it at the moment."

"Have you had any more women, apart from me, with this problem?"

"Another two ladies."

As soon as I arrived home the computer was switched on, the website of the 'committee' was easily found and the forms quickly downloaded. It all looked pretty straightforward and I couldn't think of any reason my claim wouldn't be successful. No amount of compensation would be enough. How can you possibly put a price on your head – literally? However, it would give me closure and would enable me to buy the best quality wigs and hopefully try different treatments at the hair clinics. How could they not award me compensation when the results of my treatment was staring them in the face. How naive can one be?

I made sure to blame my treatment and not the drug company as I knew it would be impossible to go up against them. Everything else was straightforward and I posted it full of confidence.

A few weeks later a large brown envelope with the committee's stamp on arrived. I felt excited but scared as I carefully opened it. The first words to jump out at me, as I quickly scanned my eyes over the page, was the name of the drug company!

"They must think that it's their fault and there is a case against them." I screamed down the phone to John. The word naivety springs to mind yet again. How could I be such an idiot?

If only I knew then what I know now but isn't hindsight a wonderful thing?

It wasn't something that was going to be done and dusted in a few weeks and could take at least 6 months to a year. There was now something else to bore everyone to death with.

They requested certain paperwork so after emailing Dr. Bernard, and telling him what they had asked for, he posted everything to me straightaway.

Then they said they wanted me to go and see an expert. This concerned me, if this adverse side effect was so rare and unheard of apparently (according to Sanofi Aventis) how knowledgeable could this expert be with this problem? Still it had to be done, there was no choice it was the first step of the process. I had to wait for the committee to contact me with a date for this appointment. So it was just a waiting game now, which, funnily enough, went on and on...and on.

In the meantime I had discovered the huge exciting world of Big Pharma's social media. I had to be spending around 15 hours a day on the PC by now, anything else was a hindrance, there was nothing else to think about. The housework, meals and having to leave the house became an unwelcome distraction.

I would create email addresses to log into forums for drugs reps and pose as one of them trying to dig the dirt on this drug.

It was while checking how many hits my 'mooning' video (on YouTube) had received that a thought hit me! I would see if there was a contact address for the famous Erin Brokovich. She was our group's hero. I had recently watched the film, yet again, and it never failed to inspire me, pushing me on in search of the truth. It was increasingly easy to believe there was something to be uncovered; something just wasn't right.

I decided to contact her and ask if she could help, not really expecting a reply. There was nothing to lose.

The next morning I was amazed to get a reply from the lady herself!

"This is amazing!" Squealing with delight as I told John. I replied giving her more information and got another email from her the following day. She said she would get one of her office girls to phone me and wanted my number. So I gave her my number, reminding her I lived in France so there was an issue with the time difference. Not wanting to miss this call I carried the phone everywhere, even into the garden when hanging the washing out! The phone didn't ring. I tried with one last email to get a response from her office girl. Yet again another reply came from Erin promising to get someone else to ring me. The call never came.

The support group decided we should create a spread sheet and collect all our info. I devised one which included everything; from what skin type we had to the colour of our hair, age, nothing was left out. The only common denominator was the same drug. There was nothing else it could be.

I started my own blog too, where I could freely rant about the knock-backs but the positive stuff too. It wasn't long before emails started to arrive in my 'inbox' from ladies all over the world who wanted to know more details and were interested in the data we had collected. It wasn't noticeable to me at the time but looking back I had shut myself off from 'life', creating my own little world at home in front of the PC and nothing else mattered. Dear friends still phoned for a chat but they must have dreaded the subject arising, at the same time feeling obliged to ask.

"How's it going, any news?' It was only after saying goodbye that I realised ninety five percent of the chat was about my damn hair or claim.

Nothing else seemed to matter to me anymore. It became almost a daily occurrence to receive personal emails, ladies from all walks of life wanting to know what information I had, what my plans were. It was easy to be a little suspicious when they asked me these questions (especially when asking if I am taking legal action) and I thought it could be someone from the drug company. Well you never know eh? Or was I just going crazy?

But family and friends did stick with me or maybe they just switched off when I talked, letting it go in one ear and out the other.

***

I had only recently joined Facebook. It was time for another idea, another master plan. My maverick (or childish whichever way you look at it) streak beckoning to me again. Imagine my surprise when I found the drug company had their own Facebook page where the public could post messages. Wow! It was like winning the lottery.

I started posting questions on their page, asking them why they were refusing to answer my letters. Being fully aware that the general public could see everything and I hoped it would shame them into some sort of response. There were no replies. What else could be done with this golden opportunity? As usual, without giving it too much thought, I took a photo of the top of my head. That should do the trick. Oh my, what was I thinking?

Before realising what I was doing that photo of my ugly bald head (minus the face) appeared on their wall about 10 times with a rather irate message underneath. I had no idea of the consequences of my actions!

The following day it was EVERYWHERE! It was all over Twitter, medical/drugs forums and blogs. My Facebook friends started posting messages under my photo blasting the company!

Sanofi-Aventis' Facebook page (Voice's) was 'closed down'. I felt proud that my voice was finally being heard but it was hard to read some of the comments on the blogs and Twitter. These were mostly made from people, once again, not reading correctly and not being able to understand.

Of course, my comrades knew what I had done and some of them jumped to my defense when there was criticism.

One of the large Pharma blog/websites (Pharmaguy™) reported:

Disgruntled Patient Shuts Down Sanofi-Aventis Facebook Page

"I actually think I did a very good job in closing down the FB page of Europe's largest drug company, something I am very proud of and something I haven't finished with yet," said Shirley Ledlie in a comment made to Social Media Intern's "Ask Me a Question" survcy.

In a previous post I documented how Mrs. Ledlie -- a cancer survivor who had permanent hair loss after taking Taxotere®, a drug marketed by Sanofi-Aventis (S-A) -- was laying siege to S-A's VOICES Facebook page (see "Patient

'Unadvocate' Lays Siege to Sanofi-Aventis VOICES Facebook Page. Where's S-A's Social Media VOICE?")

In a quick visit to the VOICES page (they had re enabled their page), I found that all the posts to the wall had been deleted and have been replaced by this statement: "Sanofi-Aventis VOICES has no recent posts." No further comments can be posted to the VOICES Wall. It appears that S-A could not stand up to the onslaught waged by Ledlie's solitary "voice" and just decided to call it quits!

A precedent has been set by this experience, which does not bode well for the future of Pharma social media.

Then another blog followed by John Mack;

"Sanofi-Aventis Updates Facebook Site with Disclaimer, But Shirley Still Posting About Her Side Effects

Recently, Sanofi-Aventis has been having problems with its VOICES Facebook page (see "Disgruntled Patient Shuts down Sanofi-Aventis Facebook Page"). I previously suggested S-A had made a faux pas because it did NOT take its own advice about posting a Terms of Use policy on its VOICES Facebook page (see "Patient "Un-advocate" Lays Siege to Sanofi-Aventis VOICES Facebook Page. Where's S-A's Social Media VOICE?"). I guess someone at S-A read my post because the site now has a disclaimer, which says, in part:

"This page is not intended as a forum for discussing Sanofi-Aventis' or other companies products including the reporting of side effects associated with the use of prescription drugs. As such, Postings that contain product discussions may be removed by Sanofi-Aventis."

The VOICES Wall is now back online with posts and is accepting comments, including the following from Shirley, aka the "disgruntled patient":

"I have just read your disclaimer... Not intended, is not the same as not allowed in my eyes"

Shirley's friends are also posting comments like "if this site is not meant for discussions why call it "voices" suggests to me you don't like hearing what is written!!!!!!!!!!"

It will be interesting to see how this all plays out and who will win this "Pharma Social Media Standoff!"

SUPPORT GROUP MEMBERS THOUGHTS

Yvonne Linssen, 44, Netherlands

'But what if my hair does not come back?' I was on the emotional rollercoaster since I heard that I had breast cancer, but the prospect of losing my hair during chemo – and perhaps permanently – made that seemingly endless ride truly a living nightmare.

I asked my oncologist this question because I had come across some posts on the internet that women had experienced this disastrous long term effect after being given a certain chemo.

'I have never heard of hair not coming back,' my oncologist answered. I have never heard it from my colleagues either, or read about it. But he should have known. This was October 2011, and the possible side-effect of permanent hair loss as a result of a certain chemo drug was known in the medical world for some years already. Even

the manufacturer had admitted that a certain percentage of women treated could experience this long term side-effect.

I had done my research and I begged, I really begged my oncologist to give me the alternative drug. Somehow, I had an inkling that my hair, my beautiful long, thick and curly hair, would not come back. But he would not budge and I did not have the strength (or possibility) to persist any further.

The oncologist in question is no longer my doctor. After confronting him with my hairless head over a year after the chemo ended, he more or less shrugged. In his opinion, there are worse side-effects. And he even doubts if the chemo is really the culprit. As far as he is concerned, he still won't warm patients that this side effect may occur....

Now, more than two years later, I am still on this emotional rollercoaster, and there is no sign that it will ever stop. The seatbelts are tighter than ever.

Surviving cancer is one thing. But quality of life is just as important. What does it take to make doctors realise this? Without hair, the quality of my life has been severely damaged. I suffer, as do the people who are close to me.

I lost myself on the day I had my head shaven in preparation for the chemo. And I still have not found myself back.

CHAPTER 8
WHAT'S COOKING?
(BRITTANY, FRANCE 2002)

We had made lots of new friends since moving to France and had had many visitors too. They would all instantly find themselves in relaxation mode after walking through our wooden gates at the bottom of the drive. We loved having family and friends coming to visit.

One of my French friends, Marie, lived at the bottom of our hill and ran a little bar/café there, mostly lunches for truck drivers and builders. The occasional rep would call in too. One afternoon, after I knew most of her work would be done, I popped down for a coffee and chat with her. She didn't speak any English at all but we always seemed to understand each other, albeit a mixture of Franglais and charades, plus it was good practice for my struggling French. She always kept an English dictionary behind the bar. During our second year here she gave us two Lhasa-Apso puppies, we called them Jacques and Rose but after a few months they became Jack and Rosie.

During our afternoon chat she said she had to go to Paris for a few days to see her daughter and that meant closing her business while she was away. Now, I don't know what possessed me but I found myself offering to run the place for her. What was I thinking! Had she slipped something in my drink? She threw the big bunch of keys at me.

How hard could it be as there were never more than half a dozen people in for lunch? I was sure my years of being a silver service waitress and kitchen assistant in Durham University would come in handy. Even though my catering career had been about thirty years earlier I was feeling confident. Well, sort of.

The day before she left for Paris I went down to help her with the lunchtime trade and learn where everything was. I already knew a couple of her clients by sight and she introduced me to everyone that came in. They all seemed to find it amusing when she told them to behave for me.

Waking up the next morning I wondered what on earth had possessed me to offer my services! Oh well, I better just get on with it. This was going to be a good French lesson for me if nothing else. Marie had stocked the fridge for the first day's menu, telling me to buy fresh food each day after that. She thought she would be away all week. My husband has always been the 'steak cooker' so that was something I now had to do. She had instructed me to cook the steaks for two minutes on each side, not a minute more. The French love their meat rare! While I was getting everything prepped the door opened and there was my first customer. He just wanted a drink and he said something which I guessed meant a glass of red wine. He didn't look surprised when I put his drink on the bar so... This gave me a bit of confidence. Just a little.

This region had a very strong accent and a lot of the older locals spoke an entirely different language than French. The door opened again and four builders came in for their lunch. After serving them drinks they went to sit down. I told them the 'Menu de Midi' and they gave me their order. They all wanted steaks! *Oh no.*

I made their starters and when they had just about finished I started on the steaks. These huge pieces of raw meat sizzled as they hit the frying pan. Timing it for two minutes on each side exactly, I placed the steaks on the plates and immediately blood started running out. It looked stomach churning. There was no way I could take that out to them so I put them back in the pan and gave them another two minutes on each side. Big mistake! They left most of it. Feeling guilty I gave them all a free glass of beer, strangely this seemed to erase any doubt they might have had about my cooking abilities. A few more people came in and everything went well. The only other problem I encountered, on my first day, was the making of the sauce for the steaks so I had an idea for tomorrow.

The same people turned up for lunch (the free beer definitely worked then) the next day plus another couple of tables. The same builders asked for the steaks again which surprised me but I would get it right today. No more free beer today guys. As the steaks sizzled in the frying pan it was time for the sauce; with the kettle boiling I measured out some of my own instant gravy mix bought from the English section of our local supermarket. Voila! They cleared their plates saying they loved the sauce and what was it! English gravy I declared.

The week passed without any other incidents and Marie was very pleased with me. In fact she was so pleased she asked me to repeat the experience another couple of times.

CHAPTER 9
FACE OFF

After pointing out several times, to the committee, that on their website it states that cases should be completed in around six to ten months, I finally get a date to see the expert. It was now ten months since they activated my initial claim. It didn't seem as though they were in any hurry. Not to worry, they could rely on me to keep them on their toes.

My daughter Mellissa volunteered to come to the appointment, with the 'expert', to help translate. Although I had tried my best to learn the French language I still struggled with it at an official level.

Because of the language translation needed, but more so because I didn't trust anyone, I purchased a voice recorder.

As the date quickly approached I was racked with nerves, in fact I was terrified. It was so bad that I constantly told John that I didn't think I could go through with it. After all this waiting, all my pestering things were actually starting to happen. The support group was brilliant, they were excited and constantly sending me messages of encouragement and even a list of what not to forget to attack them with. They told me to imagine them willing me on when confronting the enemy.

Appointment day had arrived. We had to wake up at the dreaded hour of 4 am to get the first flight up to Paris. Not getting much sleep, as nerves were getting the better of me, it was difficult to get out of bed. My nerves were made even worse with the added stress of having to fly!

"You better get up or you will be rushing to the airport."

"John, I can't go, I really don't think I can do this."

"Just get up and get on with it, this is what you have been fighting for."

I went into my Mellissa's bedroom to wake her to discover she didn't feel well!

"I can't go without you! Once you have got up you will feel a little better I am sure."

She dragged herself out of bed and off we went to the airport. By the time we were taxing down the runway to take off she had deteriorated. She could hardly speak and her face was turning scarlet. I felt so guilty dragging her along with me but what else could I do at 04.30. Was this a bad omen for today's meeting?

By the time we had landed she could hardly get out of her seat. I just didn't know what to do. I couldn't cancel this meeting but knew my French wasn't going to be good enough.

"What do we do? What do we do Mellissa?" Trying not to panic I couldn't think straight.

Walking through Orly airport, propping her up, we called in at a pharmacy and bought a few things for her.

"I can't do this mum, I need to lie down." She croaked. There was nothing else for it.

We checked into a hotel at the airport, telling reception it was just for a few hours and booking a taxi to pick us up at 13.00. Opening the bedroom door she collapsed into a heap on her bed, I put the kettle on so she could have her drink of lemon with paracetamol. She drank it and fell into a deep sleep. I lay on my bed, by now feeling sick with worry and nerves, just praying for this day to end.

The alarm woke me up at 12.30 and, jumping out of bed, I went over to her side.

"You will be able to have another paracetamol drink in half an hour and hopefully that will keep you going through the afternoon." I was feeling dreadful at dragging her here to do this for me but we were here and we had to try to get through it.

The taxi arrived and I handed him the paper with the address. As there was also going to be a lawyer there from the Sanofi Aventis it was easy to feel panic welling up. Had I bitten off more than I could chew? For the first time in the last three years I started to doubt myself. I started to feel as though I would be out of my depth with the lawyer, but it was vital to stay focused.

We drove past the Eiffel Tower, Champs-

Élysées and the Stade de France. The traffic was bumper to bumper as we drove through the suburbs, past parks and stopping at every traffic light; I kept my eye on the taxi meter wondering if he was taking us the long way round!

Our taxi pulled up outside one of the many entrances to the large imposing grey building. After paying the driver fifty five Euros we walked around trying to find the entrance that matched the one on the letter I clutched in my sweaty hand. Once inside we followed the instructions, again in the letter, down a few corridors and then up in a lift.

Because of my normally appalling time-keeping, I had made sure the taxi was ordered to get us here with plenty of time to spare, especially as we didn't know what the traffic would be like. Stepping out of the elevator we found ourselves immediately in a tiny waiting room. It was just a few chairs outside a door to be honest. The plaque on the first door indicating we were in the right place. There was almost an hour before the appointment time! That would be a first for me.

I took the voice recorder out of my bag and started to test it. Mellissa just sat there not wanting to speak, trying to conserve her energy for whatever it was that lay ahead of us that dreaded afternoon.

The elevator suddenly roared into life! The light started to move up and stopped at our floor.

"Oh my God I wonder who this is?" My stomach started to churn. The door opened and out walked two women and a man. After saying 'Bonjour' to us they sat down opposite. As there were three of them I assumed they were nothing to do with us and because they didn't have to look at the door plaque, assumed yet again, they had been there before. Mellissa was trying to listen to their conversation, whispering to me that they were, in fact, from Sanofi-Aventis! So the drug company had sent three of them, obviously wanting to crush me at the first opportunity. Not able to stop myself taking sideway glances at them my daughter nudged my leg and scowled at me.

"Stop staring at them." Her face had started to turn pink again and I was reminded how sick she was feeling.

As they carried on chatting, Mellissa was straining to hear.

"They all work for the drug company, but they are discussing another case, not yours." If they thought I was coming to this appointment on my own then how's that for intimidation! Suddenly feeling puffed up, after all if they think it is necessary to send three, isn't that a compliment? I suddenly felt the will of my comrades, all their strong positive vibes shrouding us. I would show them who was intimidated.

My fighting spirit had returned, I carefully placed my voice recorder at the top of my opened handbag and switched it on.

SUPPORT GROUP MEMBERS THOUGHTS

Maureen -Boston

I have not got my hair back since my chemo and have been through so many things. My self-esteem is down very low and before this I was always confident in my looks. I have to work in public at a University in MO and I feel like the students and all the public stare at my head. It is the first thing I think of in the morning and see and unless you have been in my shoes. Yes, I am Alive but a part of me is dead. I am single and have not had a date since this has happened and before this I was dating alot. This has aged me 20 years and for over 5 years it's been a struggle. I try not to think of it so I stay in and watch alot of TV so that I can escape from it. If I did not have to work I probably would not get out much at all. Losing my breast was nothing compared to this, my breast was rebuilt but I cannot rebuild my head and I have had to invest alot of money in trying different things on my head from hair pieces to solutions. This is my story.

***

<u>Anon</u>

I don't think the oncologists have any clue what this does to a woman. They are so intent on quality of life and eating right and exercising, and not worrying about the cancer coming back, but they don't care if we look in the mirror every day and want to jump off the nearest bridge!

***

<u>Anon</u>

Whatever we have lost - not just hair - but our history, confidence, innocence, whatever, it doesn't just go away. We feel betrayed, the whole package.

CHAPTER 10
ALLEZ! ALLEZ!
(BRITTANY, FRANCE 2003)

Not everything about living in the French countryside was rosy. Many expats, including ourselves, didn't like the hunting season. In fact we hate it. La Chasse (the hunters) think they are a law unto their own, which I suppose is partially true! They do seem to have a lot of clout. Unless you live in a city or the middle of a town, chances are, you have a bit of land. When you have land you usually have some animals whether it's cats, dogs or chickens, like in our case, donkey, chickens, 4 dogs, 2 cats, rabbits etc. There are always people trying to find homes for abandoned pets, saving litters of kittens from drowning and dogs dumped in the middle of nowhere. It is the easiest thing in the world to help.

A lot of our friends had goats; they were popular to help keep grass down, supposedly, and hedges trimmed. From the state of some of the gardens I don't know if that really worked as they seemed more interested in escaping. A house down the road from us had two very cute golden Egyptian goats. I would often find them in our car park, eating my much loved plants, and usually taking me an hour to coax them out and return them home. It was usual to drive past their home to see them both curled up on top of the gatepost's like a couple of giant gargoyles. A lot of the people I knew either had horses, goats, geese or chickens having them free range, just getting them in at night.

There are laws about how close to buildings and houses La Chasse is allowed to shoot in but in reality...

When you see them walking out of a bar with their shot guns thrown over their shoulders after being in there for an hour or so, well, it doesn't exactly fill you with a lot of confidence. There are some ways to protect your land from the hunters but it's not easy and of course being in France we all know how they love their paperwork.

You could go through all the red tape to claim your land is protection for birds, they give you signs to put all around your border prohibiting hunting but I only know of one person that's gone to all this trouble. Instead I used to go out with my big walking stick, wellies and a very irate face shouting in my best French accent 'Allez, allez' to them as I would run down the hill to where they would normally cross. After two consecutive years of this behaviour they would give our fields a wide berth.

Very occasionally I would see them walking through the very bottom of the field to get to the next one owned by our neighbouring farm. I certainly never saw them shooting while on our land but of course along with them came their damn dogs! Sometimes they were more of a problem than the men with guns. Out of nowhere you would suddenly hear a terrible noise only to find a pack of Breton Spaniels going berserk in your garden. We had several friends who lost their cats in this way. You could hear their horns getting louder the closer they got, so I would make sure all our animals were in or secured: it's not easy if you happen to be out as you might be coming home to the terrible sight of your favourite moggy's intestines scattered over your garden.

One Wednesday morning, I had been to our local market for a wander around and having met up with some friends for a coffee, I then decided to walk over to the animal section. I had purchased several of the brown hens from them before and they rewarded us by being reliable layers. If they laid too many we would place the eggs on a chair just outside our driveway, with a little box for people to drop some money in – just whatever they wanted to pay. It worked well as we always had more than we needed even after providing breakfast for our B&B guests.

They had the usual hens and rabbits when I spotted some quails. Thinking quails eggs might be a hit with our guests I bought a couple of them. When I got home I put them in with the rabbit and guinea-pig, they had a lovely open run with their secure sleeping quarters. After a couple of days they seemed really settled and were getting on with each other. I clipped their wings and after a couple of weeks they started to lay their tiny beautiful eggs. One of the quails and the guinea-pig seemed to have forged a beautiful friendship and were always next to each other, it was very touching to see them together.

Early one morning I went to let them out into their run to find one of the quails had a damaged leg, being completely bent I knew nothing could be done. Now, there is no way I could kill an animal, not even if it was in pain so I placed her in the cats travel box. Then walked down the road to Anna who had been a farmer's wife for many years, handing her the box explaining what had happened. I asked her if she wouldn't mind killing the poor little thing as quickly and painlessly as possible. She said she would take care of it and took her out of the box, I stroked her and said goodbye before walking home with the empty cat box.

Three months passed and we had some new additions to the ever increasing family. For my birthday I had been given two ducklings. They were very sweet but boy can they poo! What a mess. I kept them in a large pen, partly sheltered by trees with a little pond plus they were close to the other animals. They seemed very happy and content. We couldn't let them run freely because they wouldn't have survived five minutes with our Jack Russell terrier, Alice.

After enjoying a meal one night with Judy and Pete down the road, Judy asked

"Have you seen Anna?"

"Not lately why?"

"She has a little surprise for you."

"What sort of surprise?"

"You will just have to wait and see but we know you will love it." I had no idea what it could possibly be but I didn't have to wait long because the next morning there was a knock at my back door.

"Oh! Good morning Anna, how are you?"

She never just popped round so it must be about this surprise. I was intrigued.

"I have a surprise for you Shirley," she said beaming from ear to ear. Of course I faked my surprise. At this she pulled one arm round from behind her back. I couldn't believe my eyes. There, snuggled in her large weathered calloused hand, was my little quail with a fixed leg!

"Oh I don't believe it Anna!" I tried to keep my astonishment to a whisper so as not to scare the poor little thing.

"How did you fix it?"

"I saw you were upset when you brought her to me, so I wanted to see if I could repair it, as you can see it wasn't impossible." It had been about three months in the healing!

We placed her back outside with her friend. After a minute or two of running round at opposite ends of their large enclosure, they were suddenly back together, side by side. They were such cute little things.

We really do have enough animals now. When they go there will be no replacing them: those were my thoughts as I got into bed that night, not realising that the reduction in numbers would start so soon.

The hunting season was well and truly in full swing. Apparently they had shot a young deer at the bottom of our road, which they were not supposed to do but what can you do when they have such a strong and powerful lobby here.

Getting up early to see to all the animals and getting breakfast ready for our B&B guests was a daily task I enjoyed. After clearing away the breakfast things and doing the school run, it was back to doing the more mundane tasks of laundry, bed-making and cleaning, not to mention any gardening.

The little quail had been back with us about a week when one morning the hunter's horns were suddenly blowing uncomfortably close spurring me to run outside to check all the animals were safe. About an hour later when the sound of the horns had descended into the distance I walked over to look for the happily reunited quails. She had gone, along with the two ducks.

I hadn't clipped the ducks wings for a while and of course the quail hadn't had hers done all the time she was recuperating at Anna's. I fled into the field looking for the three of them but there was no sign, no feathers…nothing. I couldn't bring myself to tell Anna.

CHAPTER 11
THE EXPERT

The door opened and there stood the expert. Here was the man who could kill off my quest for justice in one foul swoop. After knock-backs from everywhere in trying to get the word out, it was extremely easy not to feel so confident.

He shook all our hands as we entered his meeting room. It was a firm but warm handshake. He was an average sized man, with a thick head of hair and he wore glasses and a white coat. I wondered if by wearing his white coat it helped him keep his air of authority. There was no mistaking he was the boss today. He cut a formidable figure. My daughter and I were asked to sit on the side of the large oblong table that had the two chairs and the drug company representatives on the opposite side facing us. The expert was head of table, of course. I was trying not to shake and to think that at the end of the day these were normal human beings who go home and sit on the toilet - the usual visualizations that are used when facing people that could be intimidating.

There was a tall dark haired, handsome man who was a lawyer. He looked as though he was friendly but I wasn't going to be fooled by that. Oh no. Next to him was a small woman that could only be described as a witch, complete with a large wart on her chin. You could feel bad vibes drifting over from her. She announced herself as being a lawyer too. Oh my, they had sent two lawyers just for little old me. Maybe this was normal practice. Then there was the third woman who introduced herself as a doctor for the drug company. I thought she looked very chic, friendly and had a warm smile. The expert was the first to introduce himself, then asked us all to do the same. My daughter's face had started to redden up again with fever. We listened as the expert opened the meeting by explaining why we were all there and what the meeting was for and what it would cover.

He spoke quickly but I could grasp the gist of what he was saying. Each time I caught the female (witch) lawyer's stare I would hold it for a few seconds and give her an insincere smile, not wanting her to read me.

All the time my voice recorder was working away quietly in my handbag.

For almost an hour the expert chatted away, he seemed in his element holding court, asking the three for clarification on certain information. My daughter would translate anything that was important as we went. The expert would often stop to ask her if she understood and if there was anything she need explaining to her. Occasionally he spoke in English to clarify some difficult medical terminology. He seemed to have a sense of humor which was very welcome and brought a bit of light relief to the sober table. I decided I liked him.

Mellissa was starting to go downhill again and as her throat was closing up could only croak. Much to my relief the expert said he would carry on in English which wasn't a problem for the male lawyer and the Doctor but not the witch who continued to look constantly agitated and had a permanent scowl. Bitch. So it became half English and half French, it worked. He started to question me, asking about any past health issues, writing down anything he thought was relevant. I realised it had to be done but just wanted to get down to the real issue.

I had to keep reminding myself that finally I had the drug company's attention and they were sitting opposite me!

My stomach was in a constant knot. Just to add to the discomfort it was fast becoming unbearably hot as there didn't seem to be any air conditioning, making it harder to look cool and in control. Under no circumstances did I want them to think I was riled or under pressure in their god-like presence. Suddenly he reverted into English.

"What would you like to say to them?" It bought me back to the present with a start, as the constant barrage of now complicated French had almost sent me into a trance. *Let's sock it to them right between the eyes.*

"I want to know why you try to keep the true figures of this adverse side effect concealed." Silence! You could hear a pin drop. The three of them first, looked at each other, then at the expert. I had their attention now! Let's get the party started. *Let's cut the crap and get down to the nitty gritty. Was that a little twinkle in the expert's eye?*

"It seems that every time someone contacts you to report that it's happened to them you tell them that they are only the third or fourth person in the world that this has happened to?" (not really knowing if that was a quote from them or just the interpretation from Dr. Bernard but they didn't deny it so...)

"Everyone gets told the same, plus, you have on your website that it's extremely rare."

"It is extremely rare."

"Sorry, but it's not extremely rare, I am part of a large world-wide support group, we are all suffering the same problem, there are so many of us." They were having none of it.

"It is rare." They repeated.

I delved into my folder and pulled out a chart that I had manage to get ahold of from the EMA after asking them how side effects were categorized into rarc, common and frequent.

"For a side effect to be classed as rare it would have to occur in less than zero point zero one percent."

Silence again.

"You say it happens in three percent." Pulling out the first letter I received from Sanofi-Aventis stating just that.

"According to the EMA three percent puts it straight into the common and frequent category," I continued "yet even on your website you still state very rare when that's not in keeping with the European classification system." They just stared at me in disbelief, for what seemed an age, before chatting quietly to each other. They were then talking to the expert who, by now, had a bemused look on his face. I don't think any of them expected this! *Yeah, bring it on!*

"The problem is we don't really know how many women have had this problem, the three percent figure comes from a small independent study." *But it's good enough for you to use when trying to make a point of how rare it is!* It was time to slap another piece of research onto the table. I opened my valuable blue folder again and reached in for the results of an independent study that was discussed at the Rocky Mountain Cancer synopsis in 2007. Cancer doctors from all over the world go to this yearly event (as far as I know) or if they are unable to go, get to see the results and reports.

"This states it stands at least six point three percent." In my heart I knew it was a lot higher. "This figure puts it at the top end of common and frequent side effects."

"This doesn't prove anything." The witch almost spat. Picking it up and slinging it back onto the table. *Bitch.*

"Well, that happens to be the same paper that YOUR company gave ME in quoting the three percent, but it just so happens that YOUR company added the figures up wrong." I couldn't help but smirk back at her. The expert, by now, was sitting back in his chair looking as though he was enjoying this spectacle.

There were all getting fed up because they didn't have answers for me. The witch was getting very agitated by my constant questioning and kept picking up the last piece of paper and throwing it back down – treating it as though it was a bit of rubbish. But I had the bit between my teeth and wasn't letting go.

"It's just a piece of paper with words on it, it means Nothing." Her voice was getting louder now. *I have her rattled.* They wouldn't stop repeating it was difficult to know the true figures. I had had enough.

"Well, if you carried out your own official study you would know the amount of women you were disfiguring!" That was it! That pushed her over the top.

She looked as though she would explode, looking at the expert for his support, but instead he agreed with me totally. *YES!* Without any warning she stood up and started ranting, flinging her arms around and shouting, it was so embarrassing, and amusing. Everyone in the room just sat, opened mouthed as she continued with her tirade until her two colleagues told her to shut up and sit down. *Phew, that was awkward!*

She sat down but still carried on ranting: by now the expert had had enough and told her to shut up.

"I hope, if you ever get cancer you don't have to have your drug!" he shouted at her. *WOW!* That did the trick. Wanting to keep up the pressure I carried on.

"So, if these people at the Rocky Mountain Synopsis knew, why didn't you do something about it? It was mentioned in the Vidal (a doctors bible renewed every year) in 2005." At this point he left the room, leaving the three of them chatting quietly to each other, while Mellissa and I just sat there twiddling our thumbs and pulling faces at each other until he returned with the Vidal. He found the info that said there had been one case of permanent hair loss recorded. One case!

"What about all these people in this study? Once again waving their chart at them, "You ignore this info? You don't update it every year with the new figures?"

They went on to explain that the reported cases were always classed as ongoing until they reached seven years. At seven years they miraculously become a permanent statistic.

So, it really was a case of playing with figures. The doctors and drug company could continue to tell their patients that they had never seen or heard about PERMANENT hair loss without being accused outright of lying. It might have been a play with words but that didn't stop it from being, well, what it really is. They were relying on the patients not knowing about the 7 year figure becoming permanent. This was outrageous! This particular drug combination had only been used in France for less than three years (for curable cancer and in combination with other drugs) so there was another four years to go before they would have to convert the ongoing to permanent. How on earth could this be allowed? This was a scandal. It was so frustrating and I thought I would combust. But I managed to stay calm, fairly controlled and firm, though I have no idea how.

I thought now would be a good time to disrobe! So, sneaking my right hand up to the back of my neck I took hold of one of the corners of my scarf and whipped it off; at the same time never for one moment taking my eyes off the enemy. Looking astonished, they didn't know where to look as my eyes bore into them. They HAD to see what their drug had done to me and what it was doing to women every day all over the world. This was a massive thing for me to do because nobody, apart from family, very close friends and doctors, had the privilege of seeing my ugly old head. Not counting the Facebook episode but that didn't count as you couldn't see my face.

The expert came over to me and asked, gently, if he could take a closer look at my scalp. It was impossible to speak, as he examined my scalp, because of the tears I was trying to keep in check; knowing it would be impossible to stop once the floodgates had opened. I could feel his fingers moving all over my head. It felt strangely reassuring, tickling mostly as he touched the fine wispy transparent hairs that protruded from my scalp in the way that the bristles stick out from a toilet brush. However, the hairs are so incredibly fine you actually can't feel them.

As my bravado had started to wane, I began to feel naked and just wanted him to finish so I could get my trusty chemo scarf back on. My tears seemed to stay pooled and, without blinking, I would keep throwing pitying glances at the three drug company employees, desperately wanting them to see and feel some of my hurt, pain and anger.

"You will need to go for a scalp biopsy," he said, "that will be the next step in the process." He sat back down. I scrambled to get my head covered up again, the tears were subsiding. *Keep going, we must be getting near the end.*

Not wanting them to leave without hearing all the emotions, the day to day difficulties, once again reaching into my blue folder to recover the list (my support-group buddies had created) to go through each and every one.

The voice recorder was still silently working away. Not remembering how long it would work for, I hoped it wouldn't make a noise when it finished! Imagining it clicking, rewinding and starting to play back! Do these things rewind? Being useless at technology but understanding it wasn't a tape, I was not sure what it actually records onto. Well, whatever it does please just keep working a while longer and stay silent.

Sitting there with the list and four pairs of eyes fixed on me. I started to go through them one by one.

Emotions

- I have lost ALL of my femininity, I actually feel as though I have morphed into a man.
- Deep depression.
- Feelings of embarrassment, sadness, helplessness, anger, despair, frustration.
- It reminds me permanently that I had BC.
- Fear, what else can be damaged on the inside of my body.
- Fear for life.
- To be in mourning for a part of my body (my hair).

Physical suffering

- Difficulty in dealing with hot and cold weather when wearing a wig - if it's so cold you also need a hat it has to be one or the other. To wear a hat over a wig is unbearably itchy and uncomfortable and has a tendency to constantly move, moving your wig around with it! It's easy to end up with your fringe at the back of your neck.
- Sleep disturbance – needing sleeping pills and always dreaming your hair has returned.
- Nervousness – having to be constantly on your guard; should anyone ring your door bell you have to go running round your house looking for a headscarf, and you can't just take your dustbin outside. All

the little things that normally you wouldn't think about suddenly are a big deal.

- Red, watery itchy eyes – lack of lashes and brows, we have them for a reason.

Social

- I have withdrawn from a lot of activities in my social life, e.g. swimming, to take a sauna, water sports, dancing, jogging and other kinds of sports is not possible anymore.

Financial disadvantage

- It has become necessary to spend a lot of money on wigs, hairpieces, cosmetics, head coverings, special shampoos, and vitamin pills.

We carried the meeting on for a while longer, mainly arguing the point that ongoing and permanent was misleading. The expert said that the hormone pills I was on could be another cause for my hair not returning. Several times I had to make the point that I had a very thick head of hair before chemotherapy, and that it hadn't even started to grow back normally for the few months between finishing chemo and starting the hormone medication. Dr. Bernard didn't want me to start the hormone treatment as soon as the radiotherapy had finished because of going on holiday. I finished Chemo in January and I didn't start medication till May so...

The meeting finally wound up, the witch grabbed the sheet with the regions study on and asked if she could take it with her. She stuffed it into her brief case and stormed out, rudely, but the male lawyer shook my hand and said,

"Au revoir." So did the female doctor and she even gave my arm a little squeeze.

We waited for them to disappear into the lift as we didn't want to be in there with them; that really would have been too much! All it would have taken was one wrong look from the witch and I wouldn't have been responsible for my actions. She could have been going home without any hair too!

It was a great relief to finally get outside into the fresh air, well I don't know about fresh but was better than the stifling heat of the office. Looking around to get our bearings, we could see the three of them huddled together deep in conversation looking serious. Maybe that's how they normally look or maybe they were just fed up at listening to me going on and on and on. Never mind.

Our taxi pulled up and we collapsed onto the back seat. Mellissa was feeling so bad, she had hung on but now it was all over she didn't have to fight it. I was absolutely exhausted mentally and physically, totally drained. We had just had the day from hell and we wanted, no NEEDED desperately, to get home.

Arriving at the airport we were praying our

flight would be on time. It was, thankfully, we boarded and started off down the runway. After being in the air for about 45 minutes, Mellissa's temperature was back with a vengeance and she decided to vomit. She was stuck in the toilet as the stewardess was telling her she had to get back in her seat ready for our plane to begin its descent: thank god it was a quick flight!

After disembarking and climbing, into the car we started the short drive home, falling into bed around midnight. We had never been so happy to get home in all our lives!

Of course I had to tell John about our day from hell. He got the reduced version of events, after which I fell into a restless sleep.

SUPPORT GROUP MEMBERS THOUGHTS

Anon

The permanent loss of hair on my head, my eyelashes, eyebrows and other parts of my body make me feel unattractive, unappealing and permanently damaged. This has hurt my self-esteem and my personal relationships. This is more devastating than the mastectomy.

CHAPTER 12
TEACHER'S PET
(BRITTANY, FRANCE 2004)

Before moving to France it seemed to be normal practice for mothers to help out with school functions, be it plays or day trips so I assumed it would be the same here. I knew in the UK mothers can be quite competitive with this sort of thing so wasn't sure how I could help out, especially as my French was not brilliant; but not wanting to appear uninterested I decided to take the plunge.

There was a two day sailing trip, so I thought they might need some parental help. Not that I can sail but thought there might be something else I could do. They informed me that, although it was a kind offer, because of school safety rules it wasn't allowed.

The next opportunity presented itself not long after. Mellissa brought home a school advert for a musical they were performing. As I am a qualified beauty therapist with experience in make-up (catwalk and photography) I asked Mellissa to speak to the teacher in charge to see if they would like me to do their stage make-up.

"Yes mum, she says that would be really helpful." "That's great, you will have to come with me to translate though." As she wasn't taking part in the show that was fine.

She said the teacher did seem a bit taken back but I didn't know if that was because they were surprised at my perseverance or because they didn't actually get mothers offering to help. Oh well, I had offered and hopefully would enjoy myself too.

The evening arrived, donning my immaculate uniform and my professional bag containing all my make-up, hundreds of brushes, sponges and remover, we headed off to the school. You know when you volunteer for something then wish you hadn't!

How scary could entering a large room full of fifteen year olds be? Very! I looked very out of place in my uniform, it was all very casual back stage and there was me feeling a bit of a......prat. As it happened, I didn't have any time to think about anything other than putting make upon the faces of eighteen teenagers with a little over an hour to get it finished. With an aching back and feeling extremely hot and flustered, I finished with seconds to spare and vowed never to offer my services again. We packed up and made our way to the exit but someone grabbed us and before we knew it, we were ushered into the concert hall and shown to two reserved seats, thankfully right at the back. The musical was very enjoyable, a great show, and the make-up looked good, of course.

The week after, Mellissa arrived home from school with an envelope for me. Inside was a letter of thanks written in English! And two free tickets for the next school Soirée with steak and chips!

CHAPTER 13
MEDIA INTEREST!

There were a few members of the support group living in Canada. One of them had also worked tirelessly on our campaign and had got one of the largest newspapers, in Canada, interested in our story! This was an unexpected exciting development for us. The journalist assigned to our story wanted to interview some of us as well as some of the doctors (that were knowledgeable in this adverse side effect) to get their expertise too. This could be the breakthrough we needed.

The journalist started her investigations, and found that there was actually some (we already knew of course) substance to our claim. She began to interview us over the phone, being sympathetic to our cause. Even though it was a subject I knew so well, it didn't stop me feeling nervous and I was slightly worried that I might say something that, in print, would sound really idiotic. After all, I was still a normal mum, a wife and was certainly not experienced in giving interviews to newspapers. It took a few months for her to gather all the information she needed before she could put it together. Finally it was ready to go to print. The anticipation was excruciating.

Early 2010 it was published! We had our quotes in the article, followed by the interview that we really, really wanted.

The Medical oncologist, who presented research on 82 patients with persistent alopecia at the San Antonio Breast Cancer symposium this winter, said "not all cancer doctors warn patients about this possible side effect. Some women look bad, they look ill, they look like they are fighting cancer. It has an important impact on quality of life."

He then went on to say that he gives his patients a choice. They can choose the other similar drug that has a very tiny risk of this side effect or they can take their chances with Taxotere® in combination with other drugs. He says that most of his patients chose the first drug even though they have to have more sessions with this one than if they decided to choose Taxotere®. The similar drug also happens to cost less. *Wouldn't you just know?* **"The bottom line is that patients have to be informed of the risks."**

Of course, they interviewed the drug company, Sanofi Aventis, but they answered the same garbage and misleading information as usual. Instead of wanting patients to be warned their spokesperson said;

"We fully understand that persistent alopecia may be a burden for patients, but still we consider

it's certainly something which is not life-threatening nor is it something which impairs the likelihood of survival."

Burden? They have no idea! Still missing the point completely that we just want patients to be told of the true percentage.

It was then time for the fall-out: all the online vile comments from cancer patients and the public who didn't understand our message, not forgetting the trolls. They get a kick out of writing comments they would never dream of saying to anyone's face. Most of the time they don't even care about the story, they have no interest but find it as an excuse to be horrible to people. These people do not have any effect on me but when reading their comments such as,

'You deserve to die.' It beggars belief.

The comments that had hurt were the ones from some cancer patients and family members that had lost relatives to this terrible disease. We all understood their pain, of course we did, but that's not what we were about. We were shouting about patients right's, about not being lied to, not being mislead. Isn't that what every patient wants?

About a month passed when CBS News online picked up on the article. They certainly didn't hold back with any punches!

"Drug company says it is "unable" to disclose how many women are rendered permanently bald by its breast cancer drug Taxotere® and the European Medicines Agency (EMA) says such data "are not routinely collected" even though

small studies suggest that as many as 6.3 percent of patients lose all their hair forever."

Somebody somewhere knew how many people have been disfigured, permanently, with this drug combination. The only reason as to why this was happening was because the drug company and the oncologists' know that if patients were warned about it, and given the true percentage, their patients would probably choose the other, cheaper, drug which takes up more hospital time. This is due to the fact it has to be given weekly instead of every three weeks. It also goes to show that they really didn't care that their patients might have to struggle to live with this disfigurement for the rest of their lives. They treated the cancer without any thought of how patients would have to try to get on with their lives and without following their own guidelines, as they were not reporting this problem. How were they allowed to constantly get away with this non- reporting of an adverse side effect? I certainly had my own theories about that one!

***

My next target was the EMA (European Medicines Agency).

I asked them for any info or data they had that had been reported to them about this side effect. They replied advising me to contact the relevant marketing authorization holder. Immediately I emailed them. Imagine my utter shock that within five minutes of me pressing the 'send' button our land-line phone rang. A very irate person on the other end of the phone shouted.

"Mrs Ledlie?"

"Yes?"

"Do NOT contact us again," and slammed the phone down! Where on earth did that come from? This went straight into my bottomless pit of paranoia.

The EMA gave me all the usual misleading info about the drug company only having one case of permanent alopecia when this drug was used as a single drug (mono agent). When used in conjunction with other drugs, (which is what I and the rest of the disfigured support group members had, which now seemed to be being dished out all over the world) it would possibly be higher. *Possibly!* I can only assume that if patients limbs started to drop off they might look into it! Well, to us there was no difference; it was still a physical handicap.

"Please note that there is a rigorous system in place to ensure that the safety of medicines is monitored (called Pharmacovigilance). If case safety issues are raised necessary regulatory actions are taken in order to ensure that the benefits of a given medicine continue to outweigh the risks. These are very varied and may include the request for additional studies. The European Medicines Agency (EMA) together with the national competent authorities monitor the safety of medicines which includes the analysis of collected safety data. Safety data is provided through spontaneous case reports from healthcare

professionals and patients in Europe which are submitted to the national competent authorities. Other data such as published and unpublished data including regular safety updates supplied by pharmaceutical companies, information from other regulatory authorities and a number of worldwide databases are also included. These reports are logged into a Pharmacovigilance database (which is stored by the EU member states and the Agency) and generate safety signals/alerts. The EMA evaluates potential signals and investigates adverse reactions.

If a safety concern arises (for any medicine including Taxotere®), regulatory action is taken to ensure the protection of public health. This may include an update of the product information to health care professionals and patients on the safety profile of the product, restriction of indication or suspension of the marketing authorizations.

Additional studies may be requested as part of the regulatory action depending on the circumstances. Please note however, that the regulatory action that is taken depends on the individual case and as such there is no set of fixed conditions which triggers the need for a study on safety concerns".

The last sentence bothered me the most. With no set conditions they can just make it up as they go along which also means individuals are wide open to corruption. What they really mean is no matter how many reported cases of an adverse side-effect they receive, from either patients or doctors, some group (whoever these people are) playing god with our lives, can decided to ignore them or not. Who are these people? Are there any women amongst them? What criteria do they use to decide whether they think it's worth looking into?

What the EMA were saying is they don't think a woman losing her hair is a big deal! It's outrageous. Furthermore, if the drug companies are not forced to carry out a study, then because they do not have official numbers, they can keep declaring it's 'very rare'. If this data had been collected by an official study the percentage of our side effect occurring would have forced the drug company to add it to the 'common and frequent' warning in their product information.

I truly believed that it was to prevent Sanofi Aventis being forced to declare it as a common adverse side effect. For all I knew this could be standard practice in the big pharmaceutical world? This wasn't good enough. After replying to the EMA with my exasperation and disbelief I did not receive another reply from them.

Further action needed to be taken. I found the Ombudsman to contact, after correctly filling out an online complaints form I sent it on its way. They contacted me asking for the letters I had received from the drug company admitting to this side effect and their own incorrect percentage. Shortly afterwards I received an email informing me that my case had been dropped because I had failed to supply them with the information? *What!* Contacting them immediately resulted in them suddenly finding my documents and apologizing for my email containing the documents finding their way into their junk folder. I wanted to pull my hair out… oh yes I forgot.

The easiest thing for me to do was to just forget it all. I had really just had about enough. Each time I hit a brick wall I wanted to call it a day.

Then a reply came stating that my case was being looked into to. This revived my flagging spirit enough to postpone my retirement for another day. It had become part of my life now and it did make me wonder about what I would do with all this spare time if ever I stopped this crusade. What was I sacrificing for this, what appears to be, a lost cause; constantly fighting a losing battle. How could I stop now? Everything I had fought for would have been for nothing. It was usually at these very low, almost giving up times, that a new member would join the group and after a chat they would tell us how very happy they were to have found us, how they didn't know how they would have survived this nightmare without the support group. That was all I needed.

***

As we lived not too far away from two airports it was fairly easy to get wherever we needed to go.

By now, John had a short contract to work in London. How exciting, I love London! And luckily for me there were very cheap flights available so I was able to go over almost every other weekend. It was great to go sight-seeing to the usual tourist spots, the shops, restaurants and the museums. Amongst the crowds of strangers on the tubes, in the busy streets I was able to feel anonymous, to feel no different to the cosmopolitan public rushing past me. I felt free! It was a welcome relief from this nightmare that had overtaken my life. I didn't want it anymore but felt swept away with it and couldn't just stop it all; there were too many people involved, too much time and effort had been put into it. I felt completely trapped. More frequently now, I did have thoughts about leaving the support group, wondering if it was keeping me in this world of baldness. One day soon.

One particular Friday I set off for the airport dressed in a big winter coat scarf and, of course, the wig.-after learning my lesson when trying to board the flight to Switzerland with just my wooly hat on! Flying was still an ordeal, it never seemed to get any easier. The strange thing about it was you feel terrified but when you look around at everyone they all look so calm and at ease, you can't understand why they don't all feel the same as you do. Every little bump was met with a grunt a, bigger bump or strange noise sent me into a panic.

"Oh my God what's that?" much to the annoyance of anyone who had the misfortune of sitting next to me, especially strangers.

Because of the frequent visits to London I told John that I was feeling confident enough to try to manage the train and the underground by myself.

"Don't even bother meeting me off the tube, I will get off at Victoria and walk to the flat." I declared excitedly.

"If I do get lost I will phone."

Going through passport control was a pain, massive queues as far as the eyes can see. A border control man came over.

"Anyone with a chip in their passports follow me to the quick desk." Myself and a few others went running up behind him. It was a long way down the other side of the hall and took a couple of minutes to reach it. He took the first traveler's passport to put through the machine. The machine didn't work! So it was back to the ever increasing queues!

I finally reached the other side of border control and headed towards the steps to go down to the train which would take me into Liverpool Street station. All this rushing around with my winter coat and wig on had taken its toll on my internal central heating system. My head felt as though it would ignite, feeling the beads of perspiration running down my neck then my back. A train had just left so with plenty of time spare, I went over to the machine bought my ticket then went into the toilets.

Coming out of the cubicle and looking into the mirror, there was a beetroot red face staring back. By now I was soaked through and longed for a shower and dry clothes! After washing my hands I then took either end of my scarf to rearrange it. Giving it a little tug, to level it up, I watched in horror as my wig took off, flying through the air like a bird, and landed on the floor directly in front of the main door into the toilets. It seemed to happen in slow motion, looking like a golden eagle swooping down on its prey. Turning round to run over to recover it I caught a glance of myself in the mirror. What a sight. This funny red face with what looked like a toilet brush for a head. Thankfully, there was no time to stare at this 'thing' looking back at me, as I had to get to my wig before anyone opened the door. Blocking the door with my foot while I bent down, I pulled it straight back on just seconds before the door opened. Knowing I hadn't put it on properly I quickly went back to the mirror to see my fringe was perched over the top of my ear. Bloody scarf! Off it came and stayed in my bag for the rest of the weekend. All this had made me hotter than ever but I finally made it onto the train, the tube, then a short walk from Victoria tube station, down the side of Westminster cathedral and rang the doorbell.

***

Just when the excitement of all the publicity from the Canadian newspaper and CBS online had started to die down we had another surprise! One of the support group ladies from London was contacted by the "Daily Mail" in the UK and asked if she would like to take part as the main feature of an article about women being disfigured by their chemotherapy treatment. Of course we were all jumping with joy; our constant shouting seemed to be whipping up media interest. This was happening just as I was seriously starting to become very battle weary and felt like hanging up my hat…or wig. This gave me the surge of inspiration I needed.

However, there was an obstacle. The newspaper would only do the story if they could have photos (of course) and our London group member didn't feel she could go through with that ordeal. If you can't go out in public with this ugly looking head how can you go into print for the whole world to survey. She asked me if I was up for it. There were a few sleepless nights toying with the idea. Well, I had already 'mooned' in my Youtube video, there had been my head photos all over Sanofi Aventis' Facebook page, minus the face, what did I have to lose apart from my pride? It was, after all, for the cause…ok let's do it!

The Daily Mail was going to put it in their Sunday version and interviewing several people including the support group member that they contacted originally. They were sending a photographer (Paul Cooper photography) over to my house, from Paris, who would spend the day with me taking these dreaded photographs. Oh how I was dreading this, even more so because it was going to bc a man. They asked me if I could go to our local train station, about 30 minutes away, to collect him which wasn't a problem. It would mean some time with him on the journey back home to chat and get to know him a little before unveiling my scalp.

The train pulled into the station at Guingamp

and we spotted each other straight away. We chatted away in the car, it was easy to feel comfortable with Paul, and I gave him a thirty minute condensed version of the story so far. He already knew the brief outline but I needed to be able take my wig off for him, which to me, was like getting undressed.

Back home, Paul started to set up his photographic equipment while I put the kettle on. Trying to think of any stalling tactic was futile as he shouted through to the kitchen that he was ready. Slowly walking in the lounge, I sat on the sofa. After adjusting the lighting it was time to remove my wig. Oh how embarrassing! Paul, bless him, didn't bat an eyelid and made it as easy as possible for me. He took photos in the lounge, the hall and some in the garden. We sat down to go through them so I could choose the ones that simply HAD to be deleted! It would have been easy to have deleted all of them. The Daily Mail had spent money getting Paul over here for the day so I felt that I had to put on my 'big girl's pants' and get on with it. The photographs were sorted and by now it was late in the afternoon, so time to get Paul to the train station for his journey back to Paris.

That was the first bit of the article done with and now I had the interviews to manage. The journalist assigned to me was kind and seemed genuinely interested in the whole scenario. However, I had to really think before speaking because it's easy to get carried away on a rant and I didn't want to say anything that wasn't completely correct or anything that couldn't be backed up with hard evidence.

The journalist asked questions that proved they had already done much research, and carried out our interviews on the phone and via email. She gave me the date that they would try to get this finished article in by. It was going to be published in the health section of their Sunday edition.

On the 14th May 2010 the article appeared. It was too late to change my mind now. Apart from me and the other lady from our support group they also interviewed two Doctors and the drug company.

"Dr. David Miles, consultant medical oncologist at Mount Vernon Cancer Centre in Northwood, Middlesex, said there was a need to "pin down the true incidence' of the side effect." "Of all the de-feminising things that happen to breast-cancer patients during their treatment, alopecia must be the most awful, so the prospect that it might not recover can be devastating."

It was encouraging to hear a Doctor, especially an oncologist, talking about it. They finished the article by asking Sanofi Aventis for a comment

"As with all of our products, potential side effects associated with the use of Taxotere® are communicated through the product label as well as in the supporting information provided to healthcare professionals to ensure proper use."

"Specifically, the labelling states that, hair loss occurs in most patients taking Taxotere®, and that hair generally grows back after completion of

treatment". "The healthcare community is aware that for some women their hair does not return." Yet again the finger points at oncologists that do not seem to want to point out this problem to their patients.

It wasn't long before the readers' comments started to flow in. Suprisingly, there were quite a few that claimed to be victims suffering the same side effect. Of course, there were the readers that couldn't grasp our message and told us, we should be grateful to be alive. Some of the comments were removed, but as this wasn't the first time it had happened (the other newspapers articles). I tried to not let it bother me. Thankfully there were many that did understand and were kind with their comments.

Over the next couple of weeks the dust started to settle when out of the blue I received a phone call from the journalist that had written the article. She had been contacted by a company in London, who specialize in a hair system that is glued onto the scalp. This allows you to sleep, shower and swim with it on. They were offering this system to me free if I would be prepared to do a follow up article for the same newspaper. At first I imagined this to be the perfect solution however, after doing some research on it decided it wasn't for me. Every few months you have to have it removed and refitted, and because I do have some hair it looked messy and it was easy to visualise the hair I have getting all stuck up with the glue. Not to mention having to pay for all the flights and accommodation to London on a regular basis. However, if I had no hair at all I might have been tempted.

SUPPORT GROUP MEMBERS THOUGHTS

Anon

No one, young or old, should have to go through the rest of their lives feeling despondent, unattractive, ashamed of their looks and afraid to go out without coverage.

I hope that you can relay how hopeless we all feel and that they have a huge responsibility to either compensate us, or to at least make the information public as to what lies in wait for those unsuspecting souls who have to go through this regeme of chemo.

CHAPTER 14
THE UNINVITED
(BRITTANY, FRANCE 2004)

Just because I'd decided that we now had enough animals, that didn't take into account some, let's just say, uninvited ones.

Mellissa's rabbit and guinea-pig were very happy in their large enclosure which was attached, at the back, to one of our barns. A couple of times she mentioned that she thought the rabbit was getting a bit thin and when she went out at night to lock them up she saw some rats! A week or two later, after she had put them to bed, she said,

"The rabbit is really thin and there are now lots of rats."

I thought she was exaggerating. The following night she was sleeping at a friend's house so it was up to me to feed and put them away. I opened their gate and took their food over to their huge hutch (an old single wardrobe), that rested against the barn wall; placing their evening meal inside. They both ran inside as though they were starving. As I turned around and headed back to the gate I glanced at their hutch and was greeted to a sight more suited to a horror movie!

The barn wall, that the wardrobe was up against, was covered with hundreds of rats running down from the guttering and swarming over the hutch! They started marching towards me with alarming confidence, staring with their beady little eyes. Screaming and waving my arms at them had no effect at all. So now I knew why the rabbit had been losing weight and Mellissa hadn't been exaggerating at all! They must have been sitting there, each evening, waiting for feeding time.

Early the next morning I was waiting outside our nearest gardening shop, ready for them to open their doors and give me much needed advice. Explaining the situation to the owner, he said that for every rat you see multiply that amount by 7. It was just horrific, why do these things always happen when John isn't here. He said with that amount I had no alternative but to use poison, I really didn't want to do this but felt I was left with no choice.

Buying several boxes but also a wooden trap I headed home and placed all the poison along the interior barn wall. I put the trap out using some cheese but at the same time I couldn't help but feel sorry for them. After all they were just animals trying to live their lives.

The next morning ALL the poison had gone! Phew! There was no squashed body in the trap; those fussy rats didn't like cheese. Someone told me they like chocolate so I tried this instead. I had to make another trip to the garden shop for more boxes of cruel but necessary chemicals, having to use it till there was poison left untouched.

The following morning I made my way into the barn and peeping around the door could see a big fat rat in the trap. I felt terrible. There was no way I could touch it so just left it there hoping to get my neighbour to get rid of it for me later that day. That afternoon I went back into the barn, not only had the dead rat vanished but the trap had disappeared too. Oh no! This was just getting worse. The dead rat's family had obviously been to collect him and dragged him and the trap away with them. It was fast becoming a nightmare.

For almost two weeks I had to put nightly boxes of poison out, with every sachet being eaten. Then one morning there were a few sachets left until another morning nothing had been touched. What a relief at the same time I couldn't help but feel so cruel.

John made the rabbit and guinea-pig a new (rat proof) hutch and they were just put into the run during the day.

If I thought that was the end of the rat problem I was very much mistaken.

We were responsible for taking our household rubbish down the road and placing it in the large bins that were emptied once a week. So, of course, this meant putting full bin bags into the boot of your car which wasn't ideal.

As I still had my yellow VW campervan it was

normal practice for me to empty the bin at night and put it into the van, dropping it off on my way to school the following morning. This is what happened...usually.

As school was closed for a week and the weather was bad, there were two bin bags in my van ready to be taken down the road. After putting the animals to bed one night and heading back through the garden towards the house, I shone my torch in the direction of my van, and to my utter despair the light picked up several pairs of familiar beady little red eyes staring at me from INSIDE my van. Oh no! Not again.

Needless to say after I had sorted this problem out I got rid of the van. And we rescued an outdoor cat. Problem was solved.

CHAPTER 15
OMBUDSMAN

Not being sure how long the Ombudsman would take to get back to me, I tried to put it at the back of my mind. It took just over two months which, I suppose, was not too bad. However, would it give me the outcome I so desperately wanted?

'You have mail' popped onto my screen. It was January 20th 2011.

There was an attachment which I speedily opened, whilst not breathing, and could see page after page of blurb.

European Ombudsman 0191/2011/FOR

S2011-131530

P.Nikiforos Diamandouros
European Ombudsman
Strasbourg 20-01-2011

Decision of the European Ombudsman concerning complaint 191/2011/FOR against the European Medicines Agency

Dear Mrs Ledlie

On 7 December 2010, I sent you my decision on your complaint against the European Medicines Agency (complaint 2491/2010/FOR) in which you alleged that the EMA erred by not adapting fixed rules for requiring drugs companies to conduct studies into the adverse side effects of medicines. I concluded that there were not sufficient grounds for opening an inquiry because you had not supplied any supporting evidence.

Since the additional information which you submitted on 23 November 2011 was not taken into account in the above decision, I decided to register this information under a new reference (191/2011/FOR) and to re-examine your complaint.

I would like to underline that it is of the utmost importance for citizens that the EMA's decision-making, of which pharmacovigilance forms a vital part, should be effective and transparent as possible.

However after careful analysis of all the information that you submitted to me, I have concluded that there is still insufficient grounds to open an inquiry into your complaint.

You will find enclosed the relevant decision.

Yours sincerely,

P. Nikifiris Dimandouros

Enclosure:
Decision on complaint 191/2011/FOR

Decision of the European Ombudsman concerning complaint 191/2011/FOR against the European Medicines Agency

The complaint

The complainant is an EU citizen who contacted the European Medicines Agency ('the EMA') concerning Taxotere®, a chemotherapy medication used mainly for the treatment of breast cancer, ovarian cancer, and certain forms of lung cancer.

The complainant asked the EMA about its criteria for deciding whether to require a drug company to carry out studies into reported adverse side-effects of medications. Specifically, she asked what percentage of patients would have to be affected with persistent sever alopecia (hair loss) in order for the manufacturer of Taxotere® (Sanofi Aventis) to be required to carry out a study into the problem. The complainant claims that the EMA should put such rules in place.

After receiving a reply from the EMA, which she adjudged to be unsatisfactory, the complainant submitted a complaint to the Ombudsman. The complainant alleges that the EMA is acting illegally by failing to have fixed rules that require drug companies to conduct studies into the side effects of medicines. The complainant claims that the EMA should put such rules into place.

In support of her allegation, the complainant argues that the failure to have fixed rules create opportunities for corruption.

The Ombudsman's assessment and conclusions

The complainant is an EU citizen. She made prior administrative approaches to the EMA within the required time limits. The complaint is, therefore, admissible.

Grounds for investigation

In accordance with article 228 of the Treaty on the Functioning of the European Union, the Ombudsman must consider whether there are sufficient grounds to open an inquiry into the allegation and claims submitted by the complainant.

Allegation, and the related claim, concerning

the lack of fixed rules that require drugs companies to conduct studies into the side effects of medicines

Elements considered by the Ombudsman

In its reply to the complainant, the EMA informed her that the Summary of Product Characteristics for Taxotere® states that alopecia is one of the most commonly reported side effects of Taxotere®.

The EMA went on to state that there is a rigorous system in place to ensure that the safety of medicines is monitored. This system is called Pharmacovigilance. It stated that, whenever safety issues arise concerning a medicine, the necessary regulatory actions are taken in order to ensure that the benefits of that medicine continue to outweigh the risks. These regulatory actions are very varied and may include requests for additional studies.

The EMA went on to state that the EMA, together with the competent national authorities, monitor the safety of medicines. This activity includes the analysis of collected safety data. Safety data is provided through spontaneous case reports from healthcare professionals and patients in Europe, which are submitted to the competent national authorities. Other published and unpublished data (such as a study which the complainant submitted to the EMA), including regular safety updates supplied by pharmaceutical companies, information from other regulatory authorities and a number of worldwide databases, are also included. These reports are logged into a pharmacovigilance database (which is stored by the EU member states and the EMA), and they generate safety signals/alerts. The EMA evaluates potential signals and investigates adverse reactions. If a medicine gives rise to a safety concern, regulatory action is taken to ensure the protection of public health. Such action may include an update of the product information provided to health care professionals and patients regarding the safety profile of the product, a restriction of indication, or the suspension of the marketing authorization. Additional studies may be requested as part of then regulatory action, depending on the circumstances.

The EMA underlined, however, that the regulatory action that is taken depends on the individual case and, as such, there is no fixed set of conditions which triggers the need for a study on safety concerns.

1 The summary states that, in one case, the alopecia was non-reversible at the end of the study (when Taxotere® was administered as a single agent). When Taxotere® was used in combination with doxorubicin and cyclosphamide, out of 736 patients, alopecia was observed to be ongoing in 25 patients during post-chemotherapy

follow-up.

The EMA then provided further information on Taxotere® by referring to the following webpages: http://www.ema.europa.eu/docs/en_GB/document_library/EPAR_-_product_Information/human/000073/WC500035264.pdf

This webpage contains a Summary of product Characteristics for Taxotere®2.

http://wwwema.europa.eu/ema/index.jsp?curl=pages/human/medicines/000073/human_med_001081.jsp1murl=menus/medicines/medicines.jsp&mid=WC0b01ac058001d125

This webpage contains the summary of the European public assessment report (EPAR) for Taxotere®. 3

The EMA also provided further information on pharmacovigilance by providing a link to its guidelines for, pharmacovigilance by providing a link to its guidelines for pharmacovigilance for medicinal products for human use (the guide):

http://ec.europa.eu/health/files/eudralex/vol-9/pdf/vol9a_09-2008_en.pdf 4.

The Ombudsman's assessment

The ombudsman first underlines that citizens are directly affected by the EMA's decisions relating to the authorization and supervision of medicinal products, including the continuous monitoring and assessment of the safety of medicines (pharmacovigilance). It is of vital importance for citizens that the EMA's decision-making, of which pharmacovigilance forms a vital part, should be as effective and transparent as possible.

Article 106 of Directive 2001/83/EC and Article 26 of Regulation 726/2004 require the European Commission, in consultation with the EMA, Member States, and the interested parties, to draw up guidelines on pharmacovigilance. The Ombudsman notes that the Guide has been created and published online, and that the EMA provided the complainant with a link with which to access it (see paragraph 12).

The Ombudsman has carefully examined the Guide, which comprises 229 pages. The Guide sets out the requirements, procedures, roles, and activities in the field of pharmacovigilance.

The Ombudsman notes that the Guide states that the assessment of risk in relation to medicines involves a stepwise process requiring identification, confirmation, characterization (including identification of risk factors), and quantification of the risk in the exposed population. Overall assessment of risk should consider all available sources of information, including the following: spontaneous adverse reaction reports; adverse reaction data from studies which may or may not be company-sponsored; in vitro and in vivo laboratory experiments; epidemiological data; data published in the worldwide scientific literature, or presented as abstracts, posters or communications; investigations on pharmaceutical quality, and data on sales and product usage. Important issues, which should be addressed in the assessment of adverse reactions, include: evidence on causal association; seriousness; absolute and relative frequency, and presence of risk factors. The quality and degree of evidence of risk should be taken into account.

The Guide also states that when new safety concerns are identified, which could have an impact on the overall risk-benefit balance of a medicinal product, the Marketing Authorisation Holder (that is, the drug company) should propose appropriate studies to further investigate the nature and frequency of the adverse reactions.

The guide goes on to state that the objective(s) of additional pharmacovigilance activities will normally differ according to the safety concern to be addressed. For important identified and potential risks, objectives may be to measure the incidence rate in a larger, or a different population; to measure the rate ratio, or rate difference, in comparison to a reference medicinal product, and to examine how the risk varies with different doses and information. In other cases, the objective may simply be to investigate the possibility of a risk, or to provide reassurance about the absence of a risk.

The Guide states that the threshold for deciding whether to carry out a further investigation into a safety concern will depend upon the indication, the target population, and the likely impact on public health.

The Ombudsman thus understands that the Guide confirms, in greater detail, the statement made by the EMA to then complainant that the regulatory action that may be taken in relation to risks posed by medicines depends on an evaluation of the individual case. There are, as such, no fixed conditions, such as a set number or percentage of adverse drug reactions, which automatically trigger the need for additional studies on safety concerns. The Ombudsman notes that this approach implies that the risk assessment takes a global view of all relevant indicators of risk, and that the significance of serious adverse reactions to a medicine is evaluated by taking into consideration all of these factors. Since such factors will vary on a case by case basis, no automatic conclusions can be drawn from any given number or percentage of serious adverse reactions to a medicine.

The Ombudsman takes the view that the explanation provided by the EMA to the complainant regarding its pharmacovigilance procedures is consistent and reasonable. The Ombudsman, furthermore, finds nothing in the legal framework governing the EMA to suggest that the EMA is required to adopt fixed rules to decide when serious adverse reaction reports should lead to a requirement to conduct additional studies.

The Ombudsman also notes that the EMA has provided the complainant with a link to the summary of Product characteristics for Taxotere®. The Ombudsman has carefully examined this document, which comprises 256 pages. The summary states that the most commonly reported adverse side reactions for Taxotere®, when administered, alone are: neutropenia, anemia, alopecia, nausea, vomiting, stomatitis, diarrhea,, and asthenia. The severity of adverse events for Taxotere® may be increased when Taxotere® is given in combination with other chemotherapeutic agents. The summary of product characteristics confirms the statement made by the EMA to the complainant by e-mail that alopecia was observed to be ongoing in 25 out of 736 patients with alopecia during the follow-up to chemotherapy treatment involving the use of Taxotere® in combination with other medicines (see page 20 of the Summery of product characteristics). It is thus clear that alopecia is an expected, and acknowledged, adverse reaction to Taxotere®, and that persistent alopecia is an expected, and acknowledged, adverse reaction when Taxotere® is in combination with other medicines.

The Ombudsman also notes that the Summary of product characteristics contains a section entitled "Package Leaflet: Information For the user". This section states that the user information must contain the following statements: "*The most commonly reported adverse reactions of Taxotere® alone are: decrease in the number of red blood cells or white cells, alopecia, nausea, vomiting, sores in the mouth, diarrhea and tiredness. The severity of adverse events of Taxotere® may be increased when Taxotere® is given in combination with other chemotherapeutic agents.*"

In light of the above, the Ombudsman considers that the EMA provided the complainant with all the necessary information to explain how it evaluates medicines, and how it continues to evaluate medicines, and how it continues to evaluate Taxotere®. The Ombudsman has not been provided with any evidence which indicates that the EMA made any manifest errors in its evaluation. In particular, he has not been provided with any evidence that the EMA ignored relevant evidence. In this respect, he notes that the EMA informed the complainant that it was aware of, and had taken into consideration, the specific unpublished studies referred to by the complainant. The Ombudsman, therefore, considers that there are insufficient grounds for him to open an inquiry into this allegation and claim.

Conclusion

On the basis of Article 228 of the Treaty on the functioning of the European Union, the Ombudsman makes the following conclusion:

There are insufficient grounds to open an inquiry into this complaint.

He therefore closes the case.

The present decision has been anonymized and will be sent to the Director of the EMA for information.

P. Nikiforos Diamandouros......Strasbourg on 20-01-2011

Sitting there reading the whole attachment over and over making sure there was nothing I had missed. Was I surprised with the conclusion? What do you think?

Well, if nothing else, it put a few people through a lot of work… and a lot of typing.

***

In my constant emails to Dr. Bernard I always asked if the study (the fifteen clinics in our region of North West France) had finished and what was the finding plus how many patients had the same side effect. They had counted another one hundred and sixteen patients! That was just in our little region. Imagine how many hundreds, probably thousands, of women this was affecting all over the world. I noted that amongst the one hundred and sixteen there was one man included in this total. It broke my heart. So much for me being the third or fourth person.

It was encouraging that it was finally being acknowledged; surely someone somewhere had to take charge and sort this out. If not it would go on for years being swept under the carpet, hidden from unsuspecting patients.

Most of the time, I felt so exhausted by it all, completely drained and devoid of any joie de vivre. My black cloud was now a permanent fixture, perched securely onto the top of my scalp. It wasn't going anywhere very soon.

Several months later it was time for a visit with my consultant, my friend Judy (who lived down the road) said she would accompany me. She was completely up to date with all the latest info and was genuinely interested, I think. She stayed in the waiting room as my name was called out.

It was the first time I had been in this new office of hers, we did the usual pleasantries and she checked my blood test results. After getting on and off the scales for a weigh in (reluctantly) she gave me a lecture about how I needed to lose weight and exercise, exercise, exercise, banging her fist on the table each time.

"So what is going to happen now that the study is complete?" I asked. She looked extremely uncomfortable and turned to stare out of the window.

"There is nothing we can do."

"What? Surely the drug company can't ignore it, this study that has been carried out by doctors using their drug?" *This just doesn't make any sense.*

"They can't ignore this!" I shrieked. She didn't make any eye contact, continuing to stare out of the window, leaning back in her chair and fiddling with a pen. *Why does she look so uncomfortable? What is wrong with her? She seems really agitated. Something wasn't right. What was she hiding? She isn't telling me something.*

"I just can't believe they can be allowed to ignore all of you, there must be something you can do?"

"There is nothing we can do, we have tried to

phone them but they won't even speak to us about it," her stare never wavering from the interesting, grey office block on the other side of the road.

"They won't speak to you? You must be able to make them; I don't understand any of this."

"Because one person suffered this side effect that didn't have their drug so they say there is nothing for them to discuss!" She turned to face me now placing the pen down as if to close this little chat.

I could not accept this: something just didn't seem right. As my appointment came to a very uncomfortable end I walked out into the waiting room to where Judy was patiently waiting.

"She is definitely hiding something from me."

There could be no other explanation for her odd behavior.

As soon as I got home the computer sprung into life, before even taking my coat off, to inform my support group buddies.

SUPPORT GROUP MEMBERS THOUGHTS

ILONA from New York

WHERE IS MY HAIR? Three years after my last chemo treatment that included the drug Taxotere® I am still bald. BALD at 45 years. How can this be? This is not what I was promised when I first consulted the oncologist who had prescribed my chemotherapy. I was promised that I would have my hair back and that my hair would be even nicer and thicker than before. Instead, every single day when I get ready for work and look in the mirror, I search for new hair growth, but there is none to be found. I have spent so much money on different hair growth products and supplements that if I added up their costs I could easily take a trip to an exotic place.

Friends feel so sorry for me that they often contribute to my hair growth product purchases or pay for my visits at the dermatologists I am being referred to. Sometimes friends bring hair growth products from all over the world just to see if any of those could help me revive my dead hair follicles. So far, nothing has worked. Meanwhile, I see other survivors with their thick hair that I know I will never have again. I cry because I am devastated. I know I will have to wear a wig for the rest of my life because it is a necessity, and although during the summer months wearing a wig is unbearable; I still must do because otherwise I look sickly and in my line of work one cannot wear a bandana or a hat.

CHAPTER 16
TIME FLIES
(BRITTANY, FRANCE EARLY 2005)

The children were growing up fast and in France they have to decide at a very young age, what career they want or at least in what direction. Nick wasn't sure and had just spent the last year working on the farm down the road from us. Because of his age he couldn't get legally paid for working. Leaving the house for his first day as a 'farm hand' his parting words had been,

"Allan needn't ask me to touch the cows because I am not going anywhere near them." He didn't come home for his lunch and it had been a long first day for him. I couldn't wait to hear his news. Eventually he turned up, looking exausted but with a smile on his face and declared, "I have just finished milking the cows!" So, after a year of learning about animal husbandry, driving tractors, ploughing fields and helping with the construction of some buildings it was time for him to make a decision. He chose to go into the building trade. So we had to sort out an apprenticeship and approached a local building firm. They offered him a three year apprenticeship; this meant he had, to work for them for two weeks out of every three. The third week he would have to attend a boarding college, taking normal school lessons and learn the trade.

Mellissa had, for a long time, wanted to work with the elderly and already completed several stages (working experiences from school) at the local retirement home. She had secured a place at our nearest college offering a suitable course and would also board during the week (starting in Sept).

With John working away and every third week not at home I was kept even busier with our B&B, Gite and of course the gardening and animals. I tried to see my friend Sue as often as I could. We would meet most mornings for a quick coffee as we dropped our girls off at school. I would still try to go swimming up to four times a week (a 50 km round trip) and would constantly try to improve on my length times.

As a lot of mums will understand there is no getting out of 'mum's taxi service' and living out in the middle of nowhere I would clock up a huge weekly amount of kilometers. Nick was also playing rugby most Sundays and that alone was almost thirty minutes away and usually entailed training on a Friday night too. I would try to fit in a swimming session at the same time.

On a Saturday night Mellissa and her friend had started going to our local night club which didn't finish until almost 5am. As there was no taxi service to use, guess who used to drag herself out of bed and drive the six kilometers to pick them up? I wasn't the only parent to do this: most parents didn't want to chance their children getting into friend's cars in case they had been drinking. It was around this time that the thought had crossed my mind that living in the town itself would be a lot easier and a good idea!

John was working in Germany and the drives home were so long he would get a flight back when possible. I would usually drive out to our nearest airport on a Friday night (after rugby training and swimming) to collect him and he would get a flight back usually on the Sunday afternoon.

Often the Saturday would be spent catching up on the list of things I couldn't manage during the week; John didn't get much rest at all. Neither did I!

The summer was almost upon us and I had managed to get our accommodation fully booked up with tourists again. Getting enquiries from potential guests always gave me a buzz as was seeing their reaction when they would first arrive into our car-park. Most guests that came lived in the cities so, to see the children enjoying our beautiful countryside, feeding the donkey and breathing this clean fresh air was very heartwarming.

In recent weeks I had noticed, when swimming, that I was struggling to keep up to my usual minimum target of forty lengths at each session. It had been a few months that I had done the usual sixty plus. In fact trying to do the first twenty had become difficult. Arriving home, it had become a habit to crash out on the sofa for an hour's rest before I could do anything at all. Maybe I was trying to swim too many lengths.

Mellissa had managed to get a summer job in a camp site close to Rennes, so whilst I would miss her, I thought it would be a good experience. Also, it would be a good change of scenery for her before coming home to start her course at college. As it was a two and a half hour drive away I couldn't just pop over every weekend but said I would go when I could having to fit these visits around my paying guests arrivals and departures.

Before we all knew it the summer was in full swing.

CHAPTER 17
MIXED EMOTIONS

We had started to toy with the idea of making a permanent move from Brittany down to the south west of France. The final choice would be mine, as John knew I had always thought I couldn't leave my medical team. Even though my consultant seemed to be keeping something from me I still had complete faith in them especially Dr. Bernard. In fact I think the whole family thought I would never leave this region. It felt as though I was trapped, the fear of change keeping me here.

Having recently lost Alice (our beloved Jack Russell terrier) I felt so depressed, believing I could still see her everywhere in the house, hearing her every time I put the key in the front door. *Could I carry on living in this house which was constantly filling me with this unbearable sadness?* It seemed to be the last thing I could mentally cope with and perhaps now would be a good time for a fresh start. Would Alice's death be the catalyst? We had her cremated so her ashes would always be with us no matter where we lived. The only other solution would be to dig her up out of the garden to take her with us!

The month following Alice's death was bleak; I didn't want to answer the phone or the door. For one month I forgot about my hair.

We had already booked a holiday to a wonderful resort in Turkey. We had arranged to meet our friends Karen and Jim there as they were flying from the UK. But feeling so low the month leading up to the holiday, I really didn't care if we went or not. It would have been a whole lot easier for me to stay at home, cry while looking, constantly, at photographs of Alice and hugging and smelling her little pillow and winter wooly coat. Only dog lovers would understand this feeling. The holiday was all paid for and I didn't imagine the insurance company would pay out for cancellation due to 'death of a dog' so the cases were packed.

Arriving at the beautiful peaceful resort, it was impossible not to instantly feel the relaxed atmosphere. *Packing the suitcases was the right choice.*

We left the unpacking until the next morning, when I laid out my selection of colourful headscarves, my wig and of course two photographs; one of the children and one of Alice. After breakfast I browsed through the information to see what activities the hotel offered. Early morning Yoga!

The next morning John woke me.

"Wake up or you will miss yoga." It was only 7.30 am and as I didn't want to eat anything before the session, I slowly dragged myself out of bed. The sun was just raising her head over the Taurus Mountains in the distance. Everything was calm, the heat haze shrouding the tops of the trees. It was going to be a wonderful day and I was looking forward to whatever the day would bring.

Walking past the tall bamboo and along the bank of the canal (which flowed out to sea), the small wooden painted arrows pointed my way. The canal which was slow moving and full of fish was also home to at least one of the Caretta Caretta turtles. I could hear the early morning splashes from the fish and saw a man with his son on the little bridge throwing something in for their breakfast. Everything about this place oozed serenity, it was just perfect. As the sun kept flickering on my face, through the top of the pine trees, I could see the yoga instructor setting out all the mats in a clearing but still surrounded by these majestic trees.

Ventakash started the session; it was only me that had turned up so it was like having my own private class. Half way through, hearing a scratching sound, I looked to the mat on my left and was amazed to see a friendly red squirrel doing somersaults. It felt effortless to go along to these morning sessions vowing to carry on when I returned home.

There was plenty of gentle swimming, good food, cocktails and great company, no one wanted to go home.

In the room was a list of treatments offered at

the spa. Having been long intrigued by the Shirodhara treatment, I just had to make an appointment, when spotting it on their menu. Venturing into the spa was a big step for me knowing full well I would have to get naked. The hotel's website said the spa is 'exquisitely decorated with traces of Mongolian History and Ottoman Culture' and based on the Kubla Khans reign in the 13th century. 'Indulging our guests in an ultimate healing sanctuary for the senses' sounded irresistible and I couldn't wait a moment longer.

The heady scent of Silver Berry enveloped you as you walk up the long winding entrance with an indoor waterfall gently cascading down one side. Giant candles, oil burners and a wall covered in ornate coloured hanging lights greeted you. It was totally captivating. Someone offered me a drink, I have no idea what it was but it had a grape in the bottom and was delicious. Suddenly, a pretty therapist from Bali introduced herself and asked me to follow her. We arrived at an enormous carved wooden door, she untied the sash to open it and we entered the most sublime room, with its subtle lighting, arched mirrors and heavy curtains, it was impossible not to be mesmerized by…everything. It suddenly didn't feel important to warn the therapist about what she was going to see before removing my head scarf. *It must be pretty obvious there was not a lot of hair underneath.* Maybe I was already so relaxed I just didn't care. Was it possible to already be under the spell of this heavenly place? And my treatment hadn't even started!

First, there was a pewter bowl, containing fresh flowers, for bathing my feet then gently rubbing them with sea salt. She then indicated for me to sit in a chair where she gave me a sumptuous head massage, as nobody ever touches my head it just felt incredible. Her fingers dug deep into my scalp: bliss. Again, she indicated for me to lie on the couch with my head at the far end next to which a tall wooden contraption stood, looking not unlike gallows, and a large copper pouring bowl suspended from a hook at the top. Laying there, looking up at the bowl, she gently closed my eyelids with her fingers, dimmed the lights, and with the hypnotic music it was easy to forget quite where I was. But I do know that laying there for an hour with warm oil constantly running over my forehead and down over my scalp was the most de-stressing, amazingly relaxing treatment I have ever experienced. It can only be described as having a thousand fingers running over your scalp simultaneously. It was almost impossible to get up afterwards; I was feeling completely spaced-out and exhausted. It took every ounce of strength to get back up to our room and that was with using the lift too. There was definitely no partying for me that night!

We were getting to the end of our holiday – back to reality and the dreaded committee hearing. I didn't want to think about it yet; I was still in holiday mode and not ready to break the magical spell.

Sitting nervously on the plane for our return

journey, with the realisation that there would be a big decision to make when we arrive home, and fully understanding the final choice was mine.

***

Two weeks after arriving home, we packed our bags, filled the car up to the roof and headed south to our new life in Toulouse. Alice's ashes were carefully placed in a box in the boot of my car.

We rented a house that had a large pool and nice outdoor terrace so we could enjoy the beautiful weather. As soon as we rented the house I informed my medical team, the Committee and the expert of our new address, not wanting an excuse for anything to get lost in the post.

With all the excitement of the move and making new friends it was easy for time to pass quickly. It was quite a relief to have some fairly 'normal' time as I felt that I had just about done as much as I could. Because nobody here knew about my problem,, it was good for my confidence. *I wonder if anyone can tell I am wearing a wig?*

Just as I was starting to relax and enjoy some lunches out with my new girlfriends and coffee mornings, a large brown envelope was sitting in our post box one afternoon. It had a Paris post stamp and my stomach churned. The delicious lunch I had just enjoyed along with good friends and the happy sunshine suddenly vanished. Ripping the envelope open knowing it had to be the experts report from our previous appointment in Paris. There were many, many pages, all in French of course. Scanning my eyes quickly over the pages of charts, tables and page after page of... French, I reached the last page: the conclusion. In the experts opinion there was no infection and while it looked very much like the typical scalp problem that is caused by this combination of drugs he couldn't say 100% that this was the cause.

A copy of this was, of course, posted to the Committee. *How can anything be proved 100%? Surely it must go on the probability?*

He must have conveniently FORGOTTEN to arrange my scalp biopsy (which he told me would be the next step and of course is on my secret voice recording of that meeting) before reaching his conclusion!

It was now a matter of waiting for the Committee to digest the experts report and to arrange my appointment to go before themselves and their magistrate.

SUPPORT GROUP MEMBERS THOUGHTS

K from the UK

How do you tell your 17 year old daughter that you have BC? I remember everymoment of that conversation and her immediate response "Will you loose your hair?" I told her it would grow back. Two years later it is still not back. My daughter still gets upset seeing my bald head as it is a constant reminder that her mum had cancer.

CHAPTER 18
GOING CAMPING
(BRITTANY, FRANCE SUMMER 2005)

With John working back in Germany, Nick getting on well with his stone-mason apprenticeship and Mellissa getting ready to start her summer job on the campsite, it was a busy household. Mellissa started packing her things to take, they told her she would have her own static home to live in; of course, she wanted to fill it. I could always take out or bring anything back when I had the time to visit. I would have even more work to do on change-over days as she had been a great help.

The tourists started to arrive and we would try to organise John's trips back not to coincide with change over weekends.

The day arrived for Mellissa to go and we packed my car, there were no spaces left, and we set off for the two and a half hour journey. After emptying the car we had lunch and then I helped unpack until it was time for me to start the journey home.

Nick was away at his college the following week so I had to manage the week by myself but it was good to keep busy. I tried to keep up with my swimming, still trying to go four times a week but it was such a struggle I found myself looking for excuses not to go; some weeks I would only manage two sessions. What was wrong? The lengths should have been getting easier and getting faster not the other way around!

Mellissa loved her job. She had a lot of responsibility but was really enjoying it which was a relief as I didn't want to go and pack and unpack again so soon. After three or four weeks I went over for the day. The weather was sunny and hot and we had a good day. We went for a long walk as there was a large lake; it was all very peaceful. I ended up staying the night and set off for home early the next morning. Nick was breaking up for his summer holidays so he had arranged with his sister that he would go and have a week there. A couple of weeks later we set off for the journey, arranging to collect him the following weekend. It would be good for Nick to have a break.

During the following week I went swimming, just once; making the excuse that there were too many people in the pool and they were really annoying me.

One evening, later that week, I went into the garden to sort the animals out when I felt a sharp intense stabbing pain at the side of my breast. My hand instinctively shot up to the pain…and found a lump

***

Two months later after surgery for breast cancer (Brittany, France October 2005).

Looking away from her cold, matter-of-fact eyes, I took a deep breath and began to read from the small, neatly folded piece of paper.

"Will I lose my hair?"

"You will lose some or all with the first 3 sessions of chemotherapy and if there is any left you will lose the rest when you start having Taxotere®" she replied.

"What about the 'cold cap', could I use this?"

"No, it doesn't work well with Taxotere® so it's not an option for you, but don't worry your hair will grow back when you finish your treatment."

After my chemotherapy had finished we sold the farmhouse, rehomed the 'donk' and the chickens. We bought a house in the middle of Callac de Bretagne only six km from the farm house!

CHAPTER 19
THE SECRET IS OUT

As there had been no contact from the Committee I thought it necessary to give them a little reminder that I was still alive and kicking. After two or three emails over a couple of weeks, there had been no reply so I wrote a letter and posted it recorded delivery. In France, this is the only way to get a reaction in many cases! Within one day I had an email from them. They were working on getting a date fixed for the final hearing.

The door-bell rang, late one morning; a couple of weeks after their last begrudging email, there stood the postman holding an envelope for me to sign for. It had a Paris stamp on the envelope! Once again, stomach in knots, sliding my finger under the flap of the brown envelope, my eyes quickly darting over every line until I saw the date. Trembling, I had to sit down and compose myself before phoning John to give him the news.

Three weeks to wait, to book flights, to compose my final words to deliver to the Committee, to find a translator and of course, three weeks to endure more stomach clenching insomnia. They also informed me there is no appeal and their verdict is final. GULP.

After finding an interpreter on a Paris expat forum, I prayed she wouldn't let me down at the last minute. Explaining my fears to her she promised she would be there for me and we spoke on the phone several times. It was important that she understood as much as possible about this complicated situation.

Flights were booked and with my file all ready, I decided that if I had the opportunity to, I would remove my wig in the same way I did at the Expert's meeting, for maximum effect. Also, into the file, went an enlarged photo of myself with a full head of hair taken three months before starting my chemotherapy.

Thinking it best to keep them up to date, I emailed Dr. Bernard and my consultant, to inform them of the impending date. I don't know why, but, in the email to the consultant, I found myself asking her to confirm when she first knew about this adverse side effect. I went on to say; "There seem to be some documents which speak about this problem before I received Taxotere® and I have told the Committee that you knew nothing about this problem until I had it. If this is not the case I would really appreciate knowing before my final meeting so I can prepare what I am going to say." She did reply quickly (which was unusual), didn't wish me luck but said;

"You were my first patient with this toxicity and I had never read any documents about this problem before." So, even though this problem had been published in the 'big red doctors bible' before I was treated, she hadn't read it or heard rumours; nor had she kept up to date with possible problems being caused by a drug she was dishing out?

Everything was prepared, everything was organised, there was nothing left to do apart from wait for the big day. My day.

June 6th 2011, my small overnight bag was packed; my clothes for travelling were all laid out, flight and hotel details were together in a plastic wallet and I just had to try to eat something for my evening meal. After setting 2 alarms I popped a sleeping pill: got to have my wits about me so some sleep is a must.

My day had arrived. There were thirty minutes to jump in the shower, put my carefully laid out clothes on and head off to the airport. Before I knew it we were hurtling down the runway, my precious folder clasped in my trembling, perspiring hands. Thankfully, there had been little time for me to get into a state of panic about flying and possibly the effects of the sleeping pill from the night before had helped.

After finding my way out of Charles de Gaule airport, which I always find extremely confusing on the best of days, I jumped in a taxi and headed to the hotel I was booked into for that night. As there were hours to kill, I was hoping that I could check into my hotel room early. Arriving at the hotel's lobby, which was completely over run with hundreds of Japanese tourists, I explained to the reception manager about my timing issues.

"Your room will not be ready for a while (pointing at the tourists which were now over spilling into the car park) but please go into the restaurant and help yourself to breakfast". Suddenly aware of my stomach rumbling, I found an empty table at the back, put down my bags and filled a tray from the self-service buffet. The noise from all the tourists was quite unbelievable but after putting my head down on the table, sleep overcame me.

"Excuse me Mme Ledlie, your room is ready now." Looking at the clock in reception I was surprised to see I had been asleep for just over an hour and all the noise had stopped. While checking in, I booked a taxi to collect me at 13.00, giving me plenty of time to get to the meeting place where Grace, the interpereter, would hopefully be. Getting my mobile phone out, I sent her an sms message to say that I had arrived and to meet her later as planned. There were tea making facilities in the room so I made myself a hot drink and lay on the bed, again setting the alarm...just in case. Before I knew it the alarm burst in to life, I jumped off the bed and noticed my cup of cold tea. Another shower was needed to wake me up. After putting on my make-up I examined myself in the full length mirror. This was exactly the look I wanted to portray today. After grabbing my all-important folder, I made my way to the reception and after a couple of minutes my taxi arrived. *This is it! Let's do it.*

The taxi journey lasted about forty five

minutes and passed most of the usual tourist sights.

"This is your address, just across the road – that large building." After paying him I headed over in the direction he had indicated. It seemed a bit of a strange place to meet as there were hundreds of office staff going back to work after enjoying their 'menu du jour'. Not being able to find any road signs or any indication of where I was, I found myself asking several people if this was the right address. Everyone shrugged and said they didn't know it! Bloody taxi driver! *Keep calm, keep calm.*

I phoned Grace and she told me to head towards a large building in the distance, which was a shopping mall, and to meet her outside the entrance 'D'. It took me about 20 minutes to walk there and even then, after reaching the outside of this large grey dirty building, I wasn't totally sure it was the right place. It certainly didn't look like a shopping mall. There was a graffiti covered bridge going across the busy road, and I assumed that was the entrance. *Please God let this be the right place.* It was a very odd looking building and it was only when I had gone through the doors that I realised it was a shopping centre. Paris never fails to confuse me it seems. Once inside, after walking around looking for an entrance 'D' I got my phone out again. No reply! By now I needed another shower and my feet were crippled: there wasn't much call for wearing heels when living in the countryside. Then my phone rang.

"What shops can you see?"

"A pharmacy, a music shop and food shop."

"Go down the side of the music shop and you will see the entrance at the end."

"Stay on the phone until I get there as I am quickly losing the will to live!" we both laughed but it wasn't a joke. "Okay, I am just going through the door now, how will I reconised you?"

"Hello Shirley," turning round I saw this gentle, kind face beaming at me. The relief! We headed off for a coffee and chat as we were still okay for time. Sitting down (bliss) with our hot chocolates and the much needed sugar, I tried to fill her in on certain facts that might be discussed.

"You will just be translating: please don't say anything unless I ask you to translate it for me as it is all too complex to understand in such a short space of time." She seemed such a kind person, a devout Christian (I really must stop cursing) and I just hoped she wouldn't be too fazed about the afternoon that laid ahead.

"We better make a move, it's a good ten minute walk from here." Standing up was excruciating. *God! My poor feet.*

We soon found ourselves outside this large glass fronted building. Walking up to the reception I felt strangely calm. We had to go up several floors and once out of the lift, down the corridors and eventually we found the next reception. The receptionist crossed my name off the long list and told us to take a seat in the waiting room around the next corner and stay there until my name was read out.

"There will be a long wait, there are people

before you and the Committee is running late," pushing the doors open, and greeting the room with the customary 'Bonjour' we took our seats. The aircon wasn't switched on (again!) and it was stifling.

"I bet they do this on purpose to get everyone tired and put them off their stride." As I walked over to the water dispenser there was a familiar face.

"Bonjour," I nodded and smiled.

"Bonjour Madame Ledlie," it was the male lawyer from Sanofi-Aventis who had come to the meeting with the Expert. No sign of the 'witch' or anyone else. *Does that mean they think they have it wrapped up and don't need anyone else or could it equally mean that they think it's a forgone conclusion I have won and don't want to waste their money by sending more than one? We shall soon find out!*

The gentleman opposite had half a leg missing. He had crutches and what was left of his leg was covered in bandages so I assume that's why he was here. Another elderly lady had trouble with walking to the water dispenser but apart from that everyone else didn't have obvious physical problems – but who can tell.

By now my stomach was in knots, there was sweat running down the back of my neck from the extra heat built up inside my wig but at least my feet were having a rest.

"We are next!" Grace whispered.

"Oh God, oh sorry," cursing again. *I feel sick.*

"Madame Ledlie?" We jumped up, so did the

lawyer, and headed out of the waiting room that was now resembling a sauna, and across the corridor and walked through an open door. There was a partition running down the left so you could only see a small seating area to the right hand side, until you walked round the end of the partition.

So, this is the committee. How terrifying! There they sat around an enormous U shaped table. At the bottom section was the magistrate with another two committee members seated to one side of her. There were around ten of them all sat there with their own pile of paperwork and each had a microphone fitted to their section of the table.

A woman (who later sat next to the magistrate), came over and instructed the lawyer to sit at the end of our table with a large space in between him and myself and Grace. We were seated facing the magistrate.

Everyone in the room fell silent... *Here we go.*

She started by asking us to identify ourselves starting with myself and Grace, then the lawyer. All I could see was a room full of eyes fixated on me as I tried to speak with confidence into the microphone. I opened my folder while the lawyer spoke, and looked down at my papers. At the bottom of the pile were the two enlarged photos of my head, one before and after shot. In the end I thought it better to take an 'after' shot just in case, when it came to it, I couldn't whip my wig off.

The magistrate introduced herself and the

Committee, who looked weary; as it was late in the afternoon I thought they must want to go home. *Well, they were going to have to sit here and listen to all this first!*

"You are here today because of your accusation against Sanofi Aventis so what would you like to say?"

"Well, I didn't actually make my claim against the drug company in the first place; it was you and the Committee that has constantly steered it in that direction. I have always stated that it was my treatment that had caused this problem." Everyone in the room gasped and looked at her.

"I have always maintained that my chemotherapy caused this ongoing alopecia and after submitting my first application I received your acceptance and someone had typed in Sanofi-Aventis at the top!" This wasn't quite starting as I had imagined but I had to stay truthful to myself and I would not be bullied into going along with something just because she happened to be a magistrate. In the beginning when I first filled in the application, I knew it would be madness to put Sanofi Aventis so I had on several occasions cited my treatment. Her face looked like thunder and the Committee was looking sheepish. But she was having none of it.

"Well, this is why we are here today so we will get on with it," she turned to the lawyer and asked for him to speak. Looking down at his documents he started to deliver. I could understand a lot, anything I didn't I turned to Grace who translated, the lawyer stopping to give me time to listen to her. It went on and on and I sat there and switched off as I had heard it all a million times. Just as I was about to go into an exhausted trance he announced;

"When Madame Ledlie had her chemotherapy it was still in the experimental phase!"

"Excuse me can you repeat that? You are saying I was a guinea-pig?" Grace looked at me and her face said it all. There was a second of silence before a commotion erupted amongst the Committee members. They were all talking, loudly, over each other, across the room to each other with one of them shouting and waving his arms.

"This can't happen to patients, this isn't right." After the magistrate regained control of the room she signaled for the lawyer to carry on. I just sat there in total disbelief. Experimental! *This had to be wrong*. I didn't hear another word he said. Eventually she asked me if there was anything I quickly wanted to add. But when Grace told her I had written something that I wanted to present she said there wasn't time and that was the end of my hearing.

"You can now all leave the room!" *What about my speech, my photographs, my plan to remove my wig?* I couldn't believe that was it, it was all over and I knew I had lost. I had been a guinea-pig!

Standing there, closing my folder (which I needn't have bothered bringing) the magistrate suddenly appeared in front of me.

"It is quite obvious to me that it should be your

consultant sat there not the lawyer."

"Yes."

I had never felt so deflated and confused.

As we walked out of the room, leaving the committee inside, the lawyer (from Sanofi Aventis) was waiting for me.

"Do you have a few minutes because I would like to explain things and I want you to fully understand everything?"

As the three of us stood just inside an empty room a bit further down the corridor, he started to explain. It was obvious he felt some sympathy for me.

"A drug will go through all the tests and then given its license. This drug was for use as a single agent and this is what it was first licensed for." *Yes, yes I know all this, tell me something I don't know.*

"It is impossible for the drug company to make studies using every single combination possible. Apart from making the drug too expensive, time wise it would be unfeasible. Doctors get together and it is THEY who decide how best to use this drug. They decide to use it off-label or combine it with other drugs. The responsibility lies totally with the doctors. A drug company will get a pill out there to be used; then it is up to thc doctor, what to prescribe it for. It is his choice not the drug company's." Okay I get that. He stood there chatting to us for at least 20 minutes which was very decent of him, he didn't have to do it seeing that it had been a total disaster for me with the Committee. He could have just headed off back to the Sanofi-Aventis office and informed them that I didn't really stand much of a chance. I hope he billed them for those 20 minutes.

We headed over to the lift with him, back through the large reception and out into the hot, carbon monoxide filled bustling street. Suddenly my feet were hurting again.

We reached the metro and decided to get off at the stop closest to where Grace lived and go for a meal. She looked weary and a bit shell shocked. It was easy to see that this afternoon had not been what she had envisaged and it had been extremely stressful. She suggested going to a little Italian restaurant where she knew the owner. We ate like kings! Devouring everything he brought to our table, I even had a beer before giving in to the weariness. I really needed to get back to the hotel and collapse into bed. After living in the countryside for so many years, it was very overwhelming to be in this bustling city: I couldn't wait to get home.

My flight the next morning was an early one so I set the alarm on my phone, plus booked a call from reception and John would ring me just to make triple sure.

Taking my seat in between two business men I felt claustrophobic and trying to keep control of my increasing panic, closed my eyes and tried to concentrate on the email I was going to send my consultant as soon as I got home.

Someone was lying to me and I couldn't believe the lawyer would to the magistrate. Equally I couldn't believe my entrusted medical team would lie or trick me into something. No, it had to be the drug company: it had to be them.

Before I knew it the aircraft wheels touched down. How I wish I could overcome my fear of flying!

As soon as I walked through the door I went through yesterday's meeting, word for word, leaving nothing out. With the computer on I quickly typed out my email to my consultant asking her if it had been in the experimental phase. Even though the Committee had warned me there would be no appeal surely there would be some exceptional circumstances?

It hadn't been necessary, before, to contact my consultant more than two or three times and normally I just emailed Dr. Bernard who would always reply the same day if possible. I waited...and waited...

Over the next couple of days I tried to get my head around the fact that someone was keeping something from me. Everything from that harrowing afternoon in front of the Committee kept going round and round in my head. Something so important, to me and the cause, and I had no clue what so ever. *What the hell could it be?*

Trying to keep myself busy by doing the house work, the house had never been so clean! Every time I walked by the computer I would look in my inbox... nothing.

Finally there was a reply from my consultant. Clicking on 'open' I took a deep breath.

"FEC100 + Taxotere® became a standard

treatment in France in 2004 for patient with node positive breast cancer, after the presentation of the PACS01 study in 2004. So it wasn't an experimental treatment and you don't have to sign any consent for standard treatment. In the presentation in 2004 and in the publication, there was no information on long-term hair loss.

Kind regards"

"Oh my God, the lawyer was lying! He was lying!" I screamed hysterically down the phone to John.

"How could he stand there in front of the magistrate and blatantly lie?" I had to inform the Committee as quickly as possible before they completed my dossier. As speedily as my fingers would type I emailed them, just one line: my consultant said it was not in the experimental phase as the lawyer for Sanofi-Aventis had declared. I didn't have long to wait; less than an hour in fact.

"The lawyer didn't actually mean it was 'experimental' what he actually meant was that when you were given it, it didn't have its licence." What! During the Committee meeting as soon as the lawyer said that it was in the "experimental phase" there was such a commotion amongst Committee members, and I was so stunned I have no idea what was said by the lawyer afterwards. How I wish I could have got my hands on a copy of the minutes from that hearing. By now, I felt so confused I couldn't think straight. This last revelation floored me. It was time to do the very British thing, put the kettle on, sit down with my cup of tea and try to think clearly. So, if that was correct and it didn't have its licence this would explain why the magistrate said what she said to me at the end.

"It should be your consultant sitting in that chair," was playing on loop inside my frazzled brain.

I didn't know whether to laugh or cry. All it took was one email to shatter all the trust I had for my medical team. The doctors I had trusted with my life, my team that I had believed in and constantly praised. They had misled me for years; let me rant about the drug company knowing full well they were legally in the clear. How could they do this to me? All the time and money spent on a wild goose chase when they knew all along that they had not carried out their obligations or followed procedures. They knew I was barking up the wrong tree but let me carry on knowing I couldn't possibly win and I am sure, hoping their secret wouldn't be forced out into the open.

It was time to email Dr. Bernard and hear it from them, let them squirm; I needed to hear it from my team to be one hundred percent sure. It was a couple of days before I received the email from him confirming what I already knew deep down.

"When you received Taxotere®, it had not yet its 'Autorisation de Mise sur le Marché' (AMM) licence for breast cancer. It means that, at this time, it had not been approved by the French Government for this use. But there were so many studies showing an improvement in breast cancer outcomes with its use, that we used it before the AMM (a kind of French FDA approval). In fact, Taxotere® received its AMM (licence) for its use in breast cancer a few months later." It was true then. They knew I had finally uncovered the truth. The fact that it had received its license a few months later is irrelevant. In those few months life threatening adverse side effects could have been reported forcing this combination to be shelved. No wonder the last consultation with the consultant was so uncomfortable for her: why she couldn't look me in the eye. I knew she was hiding something and now I knew what that something was.

***

A couple of weeks later the decision from the Committee arrived. It was short and to the point. Two pages informing me my claim had been unsuccessful; even though it was expected, it was still like a kick in the stomach to read it in black and white. However, when I reached the last paragraph there was a life-line thrown in! As they had already informed me there was no appeal facility this was a surprise: a very fine life-line but one none the less. They presented me with the opportunity to ask for conciliation with 'someone' who I felt was responsible. Because of the magistrate pointing out it should be the consultant sat in front of the committee I could only assume this is the person they now thought I should put forward. *You are damn right, I will.*

It was easy enough; I just had to inform them I would like to have conciliation with the consultant. Off it went in the post. I soon received an acknowledgment of my request and they briefly outlined the procedure. The Committee now have no further contact with me and my case with them is closed. I would be contacted by an independent lawyer, in Paris, who would arrange a meeting with the consultant and me, again in Paris, and the lawyer would make her decision and pass it onto the Committee. This felt a positive move because no matter what the consultant may say she couldn't deny she didn't inform me that they were using it off label: that it did not have its licence to be used combined with other drugs. Plus there were other accusations from me. After doing some more research about the protocol for prescribing off label chemo, I came across a doctor in France who wrote a paper about this topic. I contacted him and asked

"When a patient is given off label chemo protocol, is it necessary to inform the patient that it is off label"?

"YES!" That was the reply I so desperately wanted. Was this applicable in 2005 I needed to know.

"Is there a 'link' or other document that I can read about this subject?"

"First, it depends on the country; in France since the Kouchner law in 2002, the patient must be informed (verbally) about his treatment whatever it is on or off-label. Regarding off-label and following the "Mediator® scandal" that is responsible in France for about 500-2000 deaths in relation with off-label use, the French law has been discussed last week in Parliament. The physician will have to write in the patient chart, the reasons for off-label prescription and some off-label uses will have to be accepted by the French drug agency." So, I was supposed to be verbally informed that it was off-label.

"Sorry I have another question. In 2005 was it necessary for the doctor to have a signed consent form for the chemo regime (off label) and should the doctor have disclosed any financial benefit for prescribing the off label chemo regime? Lastly is the doctor obliged to also offer an 'on label' alternative?"

"Where are you from? From the French point of view, no signed consent or any financial disclosure was necessary in 2005. Off-label treatment is generally offered when on-label is impossible (no agent labelled for the type of clinical situation, co-morbidities that prevent the on-label chemotherapy, no possible inclusion in a clinical trial)."

With this new information I started to build a new dossier for the conciliation. As far as I was concerned the consultant didn't have a leg to stand on.

A friend asked me, recently, what it was I was hoping to achieve from this new action. Thinking about the answer thoroughly and truthfully took a minute. To get the closure I so desperately needed, that I had to take it as far as possible and felt that I would know when the time was right to put an end to it. There was also the need for a massive, groveling apology from her, for her to take the time to appreciate this devastating disfigurement and to inform her future patients that it is a very real possibility and not dismiss it as very rare. Very rare it most definitely is not! I also wanted some financial compensation that would pay for any hair loss treatments and to enable me to buy the best wigs, for the rest of my life. Oh yes, let's not forget a wrap across the knuckles for not following procedures. Then I would be ready to finally move on.

About a month passed until I received the conciliation letter from a female lawyer in Paris. The date was for September, it included the time and address. I confirmed this date was good for me. About two weeks before the date I booked my flight. Instead of booking another hotel for that night I managed to get a seat on the very last flight out of Paris, it would save on the ever increasing costs that were building up. My new dossier was completed; I was feeling ready and extremely confident, for once.

The afternoon before my conciliation I started to prepare my power outfit and paperwork when the doorbell rang. It was the postman, he handed me a recorded letter with a Paris post stamp. As there was nothing due I had no idea what it was...

Once again I found myself screaming down the phone to John!

"It is cancelled! It's cancelled! Oh no, I can't believe it. It has been cancelled because the consultant has not responded to the lawyer's letter so the meeting is off" I yelled. Apart from the fact I was furious with the consultant, it was the extra expense of losing the flight money. *What an absolute bitch.*

My friend Maggie, who was helping me, contacted the lawyer who said she would try to organise another meeting and told me not to book my flights until the consultant had confirmed; if she confirmed. She asked me if the next available date was good for me, which it was, so said she would contact the consultant and she would get back to me. "If she agrees to the next date, there is nothing to stop her just cancelling on the day while I am up in the air on that early morning flight," I wearily said to John.

"Let's wait and see."

Later, she broke the news to me that the consultant was refusing to take part in the conciliation full stop and there was nothing she could do to make her attend. She was, therefore, forced to close my case and forward it to the Committee so they were aware of the situation. *So what do I do next? I needed to think about it for a day or two.*

Everything I tried to do just didn't get anywhere. It all just felt so unjust and I knew that there were other women being dragged into my world every day. They had the right to know.

I came to the conclusion it had to be given one last shot. The magistrate's words wouldn't leave my head "It is obvious to me it should be your consultant sitting there not the lawyer from

Sanofi-Aventis." Right, I would make a fresh claim against her; forget the conciliation, a new Committee application. They couldn't refuse it, surely, after what the magistrate said.

It was like ground hog day, downloading the forms and painstakingly going through each section, finding all the relevant paperwork making sure all the T's were crossed and I's dotted. Off it went in the post.

Several weeks went by when my longed for brown envelope was delivered. Sitting down to open it, so sure it was just going to be an acceptance and then the long wait would begin all over again, after all, what the magistrate said to me almost seemed like an invitation. Disbelief and shock jumped out at me from the envelope. No! No! No! This can't happen how can they refuse it? I was so distraught by now and the realisation hit me that I was fighting a losing battle. If they all close rank what can you do? Nothing.

Maggie helped me compose a reply to them.

"I would like to know why you only take into account Article L 1142-1 of the Health Code. There is also an Article concerning the non-respect of my free and informed consent (Articles 35, 36 and 41). Why doesn't the Committee take into account that I was not sufficiently informed of the treatment prescribed? Can you confirm that a doctor has no obligation towards a patient who has to have treatment after breast cancer, i.e. he is not obliged to say that the treatment has not yet received the AMM (licence), and he doesn't have to propose another treatment which has already had the AMM?" Within days I received their answer. Just a couple of lines informing me they would not be answering any questions from me and that my file was completely closed. I was consumed with hatred.

SUPPORT GROUP MEMBERS THOUGHTS

Pamela Kirby

I dropped out of the group that we had formed because despite hundreds of phone calls and letters to cancer researchers, breast cancer specialists, news reporters, universities, and major cancer treatment centers women were reporting the same conditions after four years of trying to get the word out - I couldn't listen to another twenty-something asking 'why' their hair had not returned as they were told that it would.

I am devastated and can't believe that we are doomed to this. I am not discounting the fact that I am glad to be alive in any way but this is a constant reminder and it is extremely uncomfortable to wear wigs all the time. But mostly, I am so sad that I couldn't keep so many other women from experiencing the same fate.

CHAPTER 20
ENOUGH IS ENOUGH

After chatting to Maggie about the latest, and possibly the last, knock-back we thought it might be an option to find a lawyer that might offer a 'no win no fee' option. They don't really have that in France but it was worth finding out if there was another solution. Maggie set off in her quests to find someone. There was a hurdle because the incident occurred in a totally different region of France, this caused added complications. However she was a woman on a mission!

Maggie managed to find a lawyer who, after a brief run-down of my story, was interested in my case and wanted to set up a meeting. As usual this raised my hopes a little.

His office was in Toulouse city centre and it took over an hour to get there. The heat was stifling and the metro was packed but after a long walk past cars stuck in the rush hour traffic, we found the address. Opening the grand old wooden door we entered a dark corridor with ancient wooden steps winding round and round, up and up. Finally we reached a door with his name above. It was almost five o'clock, we rang the bell, nothing; we rang it again, still nothing and door was locked. We sat on the old wooden steps and waited. Five minutes...ten minutes...twenty minutes, where the hell was he?

"How long are we going to wait?"

"Let's give him five minutes more". A door opened below, sounding like the ground floor, and we could hear long laboured footsteps coming up each floor.

"If this isn't him I am not waiting any longer!" then appearing in front of us was this little bald man from Gaudaloope, with a dickie bow tie and both hands full of shopping bags. He proudly declared he had been shopping in the sales and bought himself some shirts and shoes! No apology. Not a great first impression.

Sitting in his old fashioned, sparse office we got started on the story; from the beginning. It was a large office with a distinct lack of furniture and anything personal. On the far side of the room was a large empty fish tank with a plastic dinosaur on the top. He seemed to enjoy the sound of his own voice, as we sat there listening to him going on and on I wondered if his fish had died out of boredom.

He was mildly irritating but because he seemed to think there was a case I tried my best to like him but it wasn't easy. He just wouldn't shut up. We had to listen to other cases he had had success with and he kept mentioning the fact that my doctor didn't make me sign anything before having my chemotherapy.

I tried to explain that I had believed I had signed something but when I asked to see a copy of it I was told that I didn't have to sign anything so assumed I had imagined it: checking with several doctors in France that this was, in fact, true there was nothing to sign with standard treatment. Several times I repeated that it was not necessary to sign anything but he didn't seem to hear.

Then the subject of payment came up; it was a reasonable minimum charge and then if we won the case it would also mean he would get ten percent of the compensation. So it was in his best interest to get as much compensation as possible. The case would have to be heard in the region that I had my treatment so this meant payments to him for his expenses, which could end up being in the thousands, it wasn't an easy area to reach and it would been at least one night in a hotel and flights. The only other alternative would be for him to find a colleague in the same area to act on his behalf in the initial stages with himself going up just at the end for the day in court.

He explained how, once my complaint was registered, my consultant would receive a summons, hand delivered, and then it would all move on from there. We had been there about two hours and it was drawing to an end – thank God!

It was good to back out into the sunshine and heat. He was going to work on my dossier for a couple of weeks and would contact Maggie when he had something to tell us.

After almost a month, and still no word from him, Maggie emailed him and he told her he would need another week. Eventually he got back to her and we went back for another long boring meeting.

Once again we found ourselves entering his over-sized, dismal office: he was almost totally hidden behind his enormous desk covered in huge piles of folders. *Does this guy know what he is doing?* I couldn't help but wonder if the largeness of everything was anything to do with him being so tiny: this didn't explain the empty fish tank though, which I found slightly irritating.

He had found a female lawyer, Sophie, who worked in the same town that the complaint would have to be lodged in, that she would represent him for the first couple of appearances. Her costs were going to be a lot less expensive than his expenses to go up there and do it all himself. He was waiting for a date to be set but it would be soon. We had to hope that the magistrate would say there is a case and then move onto the next step. Even though I still had doubts about this 'lawyer' I had to try to put them to the back of my mind because there wasn't anyone else and according to him he had be successful on other medical cases: maybe he would surprise me? The meeting only lasted an hour this time so that was a relief. He would contact Maggie soon with a date for the first hearing but would also continue to work on my dossier and needed me to give him more paperwork. Everything he asked for he got within twenty four hours. The rest was now up to him, there was nothing left for me to do.

Two or three weeks went by when Maggie informed me she had heard from him and the date had been set!

At the previous meeting with him he told us that at least a week before the first magistrate's appearance he would email me the file he had composed and I would go through it with a fine tooth comb to make sure it was totally accurate. So, with a little over two weeks to go it should arrive any day. I waited but nothing came. With just one week left I had begun to panic.

"Where is it Maggie what is he playing at? He can't pass this on to Sophie until I have checked it."

"I have tried ringing him but there is no reply, so, I have left a message on his secretary's machine but I have also sent him an email," Maggie said.

"Sophie also needs time to go through it before the actual morning she has to present it." I could hear a familiar resigned tone to my voice.

More days passed, still no reply, more emails to him were sent and more phone calls to his secretary who said she had passed the messages on. It was now the day before the hearing and I was totally clueless at what this stupid man was doing.

"The secretary said she has passed my messages on to him so I don't know what he is playing at but I will phone again after lunch."

"Okay Maggie can you please tell his secretary

to tell him if he isn't interested in the bloody case, to stop messing around and just say so and he can refund the cheque." I was livid! Maggie phoned back after lunch and passed on my message. Well, that got a reaction. Within minutes he had emailed Maggie, telling her that nobody speaks to him like that and my cheque was in the post! He also said that he was enclosing an article he had found the previous week (all he had to do was explain) with the new directives that had been brought in to make it easier for patients to win their compensation claims: but of course, as it was now easier the compensation was ridiculously low.

One case of a man, who had lost the use of his manhood permanently, had been awarded two thousand Euros! Now, in France, if that's all he got for that, I would have received about a quarter if I was lucky! Not even touching the costs of everything up to now. He said he would have approached it differently because of this directive but because of my rudeness he was cancelling my contract with him.

So, he didn't seem to think that leaving us totally in the dark about what was happening and not even having the courtesy to reply to any of the messages to explain was rude! I was spitting feathers.

A few days later when I had calmed down I contacted this other lawyer, Sophie, and explained that I was looking for a new lawyer and would she be interested plus would she be able to do the same payment agreement of a basic fee plus 10 percent of the compensation. She replied quickly saying that she would definitely be interested and wanted to organise a meeting.

"We are going on holiday for a couple of weeks and I will contact you when I get back if that's okay?" It was fine with her.

Did I really have any fight left in me? I wasn't sure anymore. Maybe I should just lodge a complaint to the l'ordre des medicines (they issue the licence to practice) about my consultant and leave it at that.

It was almost holiday time, we were going back to the wonderful resort in Turkey again so decided I would not think about it until I returned. I had one of my best friends coming to visit the following week so I just wanted to enjoy my time with her.

Beckie arrived, with her boyfriend, and it was so good to see her: it had been way too long. We had so much to catch up on. The next few days were filled with sunbathing, messing around in the pool, enjoying BBQ's and sitting at the table eating masses of chocolate (that she had bought in duty free) and drinking gallons of mint tea. Catching up on absolutely everything: of course I brought her up to date with the hair scenario but I didn't really want to dwell too much on it as I didn't want anything to dampen the short time we had together. Beckie had been busy herself, not only with her amazing beauty salon she runs with her partner but she had started a charity.

She has a close family member who has been fighting a gynaecological cancer, I had met her once, and had kept up to date with her condition.

The radical treatment she was having was ...unbelievable...horrific. Sitting there listening to what this young woman was going through was unimaginable. Beckie had set up a charity 'Bright Tights' to try to raise awareness about these cancers that are not usually talked about. As we chatted I suddenly felt... guilty. Before, when strangers made comments on forums or the comments section of newspaper articles I was involved with, telling me I should be grateful for being alive, I dismissed them as not understanding my message. This was still true, at the end of the day it was my life and it was my message; but hearing Beckie telling me all this started to make me feel...ashamed.

A day or two after Beckie went back home, looking tanned and gorgeous, John came home from his short working trip to India. As we got into bed that night I told him some of what Beckie had said. He was shocked too and I promised John I would never, ever, moan about my hair again. Ever!

SUPPORT GROUP MEMBERS THOUGHTS

Karen Robinson

I always thought my hair would grow back after Chemo. Everyone said so. My only thought was will it be straight or curly! Little did I know it would not return. People say "at least you are cancer free," but I feel like I am a perpetual cancer patient stuck in a limbo unable to go back to a "normal" way of life again and I am sad and angry at the same time.

CHAPER 21
A NEW DAWN

Our suitcases were packed and we were ready to go back to our favorite place! All that was left to do was to throw in my trusted old wigs and some headscarves at the last minute. Just because I had taken a vow never to moan about my hair again didn't mean that my sight was impaired: I could still see my reflexion in the mirror, it was still a depressing vision that greeted me. At least there was no more verbal moaning about it to everyone, how relieved must they all be!

Having looked into driving to the resort instead of the dreaded flying meant a week extra travel and extra time off work, making it out of the question. We were finally on our way.

As soon as our taxi pulled in through the gates of the resort it was back to total relaxation mode. We had arranged to meet our friends there but we had a few days on our own before they all arrived. The following morning, after breakfast and leaving John on the sunbed I had a walk around some of the gardens. The place is just so peaceful; there is something so special here I can't quite put my finger on it. It is like this warm, secure protective barrier that wraps itself around you, nothing else matters and you can see it has the same effect on everyone else staying there. The flora is stunning with Callistemon (bottle brush) in the most striking colours, masses of Birds of paradise grouped together and no shortage of the heavenly aroma of Jasmine. It was intoxicating.

As we went into the hotel for lunch, walking past reception, we stopped to read the information, and I was happy to see they were offering Yoga again. Only this time it was different. Instead of the one hour session, they had thirty minutes of breathing and mediation followed by an hour of Ashtanga yoga. This sounded intriguing and I couldn't wait till the next morning.

After a relaxing day of swimming and eating healthy delicious food we decided to have an early night, as it had been a very early start to the day before, and took us fifteen hours to reach the resort in total. Hanging around in airports for connecting flights took up most of the time. Plus I couldn't wait for the following morning to try out this new yoga session.

The following morning, we were up early and I donned my yoga outfit and put my wig on. With the headband feeling secure (I had a new wig that was attached to a headband) I thought it would be strong enough to keep it in place even for the downward dog!

Once again, I enjoyed the early morning walk to the special place amongst the pine trees and squirrels. Meandering past the now familiar bamboo running along the sides of the canal, I could see the clearing and someone placing the mats out. As I approached the little bridge, I could just make out someone else and not the little Indian yogi, eventually realising it was the manageress of the spa. That was a surprise. She recognised me and I told her I was surprised to see her there. After having been so used to the Indian man giving these sessions I felt unsure about the manageress (Marites) taking over but it could be interesting.

We sat on the mats and waited a few minutes but nobody else turned up. So we began. She started by telling me, in her beautiful Filipino accent, about her time in a yoga retreat in Italy, how she felt when she arrived and her emotional journey whilst there. Her voice sang to me; it was beautiful, suddenly feeling rather emotional myself. She then talked about her visit to the yoga instructors retreat in Thailand. We then began with the breathing and meditation. Time seemed to stand still and it felt like we were the only two people on the planet: we then started an hour of yoga. It was tough and it took every ounce of strength to manage every pose but at the same time it felt energising and quite euphoric. After the session finished I wandered back to find John and had a quick swim before breakfast. I felt so invigorated!

The next morning another lady joined us. This

session was just as uplifting even with aching muscles from the day before. Some of our friends were arriving the next day so we were excited about seeing them. Almost as soon as they arrived I tried to talk Yvette into coming to yoga with me the next morning. She agreed to have a go but not the breathing and mediation. There were more ladies the following day and as before she started with her emotional, spiritual talk. I really looked forward to this, each day, not really remembering what she spoke about but it felt soothing and I felt almost trance-like. At the end of the session the last pose was to lay down flat with arms and legs away from the body and just rest: aptly named the corpse pose. I could hear her moving from one mat to another, spending a minute at each one. Almost asleep, and feeling thoroughly relaxed, I was aware that she was kneeling down behind my head. The next thing her hands were massaging my head, my wig! She would have felt all the ribbons and gaps in it knowing instantly this wasn't my scalp. I didn't care: I didn't care one single bit! Her hands seemed unjudging as if they didn't notice it was a wig and if it was, they weren't wondering was I wearing one.

It was time to get back to reality and pack our bags as our last day arrived. Feeling so happy and content I really did not want to leave. Waking up and wandering back through the gardens for my last yoga session felt both happy and sad. Putting everything I had in to the session, and finally at the end, lying in the corpse pose, my eyes closed. After several ethereal minutes it was time to gradually open my eyes. I gazed up, finding my way through the tree tops to the clear blue sky beyond. Slowly standing up and rolling up my mat and feeling very different. Strolling back to John it occurred to me what this feeling was. I felt at home in my own skin.

Looking up at the sky all the way over to the horizon there was no sign of my black cloud.

AFTERWORDS

After returning home from that last holiday feeling so different, so comfortable in my own skin has had a huge effect on my life: I am sure my family's too. These feelings have lasted almost a year now and I am confident they will stay with me. It had been seven long years since discovering I was going to have to deal with this disfigurement. Having to find a way to cope, not only the physical aspect, but also the mental torment that is with you every minute of the day and night. I have been so very lucky. I have asked myself if what happened to me was an epiphany and I think it probably was. Hopefully, this book will give some encouragement to others. If you have been affected from the same treatment as me you owe it to yourself and to others to make sure your case is reported. This problem can't be ignored forever. Never be afraid to shout from the roof tops if you have to! But don't become so obsessed to the point that it closes your mind to the rest of your life. If you are affected by something else I hope you find your peace, never give up hope there is something out there, somewhere, to help you. You can stumble across it when you are least expecting it.

You are beautiful.

A CONTRIBUTION WRITTEN BY DR. HUGUES BOURGEOIS

Are we whistle-blowers? I've been wondering about that ever since I listened to a programme on the subject on France Culture: «good faith and public interest ».

In 2008, my colleague, Dr Françoise Grudé, and I highlighted a delayed effect from a drug used in the remedial treatment of breast cancer: Taxotere®, manufactured by Laboratoire Sanofi-Aventis. The undesirable effect was not only suboptimal hair regrowth - it also concerned integument (eyelashes, eyebrows, pubic hair and nails). In December 2009, we attended one of the main conventions on breast cancer (San Antonio Breast Cancer Symposium) where we made a presentation on more than one hundred cases of persistent alopecia colligated in less than two years in Brittany and the "Pays de la Loire" region.

About 48,000 women get breast cancer in France each year and many of them will be treated with this chemotherapy which is still the standard treatment in France and internationally.

We have continued our work in order to support our statements and this year we propose to make a presentation at an American convention. It concerns a study (ERALOP) carried out in 2012 with the help of the drug monitoring department of the University Hospital of Angers. A questionnaire was sent out to more than 800 patients treated for breast cancer in 2008 and 2009 in five centers in Northwest France. 80% of the patients returned the questionnaire and we can confirm that a third of them report incomplete or partial hair regrowth.

Time goes on, and more women are treated every week with this standard protocol but other therapeutic alternatives exist which are just as efficient, or adjustments in the nursing care could be implemented (use of a cold cap, see the ALOPREV study).

Convention on cancer. So what should we do? We are going to make presentations at two major American Conventions on cancer: one in Chicago in the Spring (ERALOP), and the other one in San Antonio in the Winter (ALOPREV). We are also preparing a film giving information on this risk and how to limit it.

But above all, thank you Shirley Ledlie, for allowing us to make this contribution to your book. Well done for your combat and your courage!

Hugues Bourgeois

Please note; the members of ASCO (Chicago) refused to let Dr Bourgois present this study even after an appeal. We are now hoping that he will be allowed to present it in San Antonio (ALOPREV) later in the year (2014).

ACKNOWLEDGMENTS

A million thanks to my wonderful family. You all believed in me when I announced I was going to put pen to paper. Thank you to ALL my fantastic friends for not telling me to 'shut up' during my obsession.

There are some doctor's that I want to say a special 'thanks' to, without all your help I would not have been able to write this book. Dr. Hugues Bourgeois, Dr. grude, Dr. Miguel, Dr. Lamezec and Dr. Guignard. Thank you Erika Bageman (Dignitana AB) for your support. Maggie, I can never thank you enough. My proofreaders, what can I say! Thank you, thank you and thank you. Lauren, Dinah and Nancy – amazing.

Front cover design idea by the talented tabathadesign.tumblr.com and Jill Coleman for modeling for me.

Marites Florentino, thank you for changing my life through yoga and being a friend. www.ourbreathingspace.com

Last but not least an enormous thanks to my bald buddies in the 'support group' – let's keep up the fight girls.

ABOUT THE AUTHOR

Shirley Ledlie was born in 1958, in Nottingham, England. She is a mum of two and wife to John. Her first success, in writing, was at the age of 10 after winning first prize for her entry about the delicious subject of the cocoa-bean. She still loves chocolate...

She didn't write again till thirty five years later, when she wrote a weekly column for the 'Bella' magazine in the UK. This continued for a year, during which time, she built up a large fan base. At the age of 47 years she was diagnosed with Breast cancer. Her treatments included surgery,chemotherapy, radiotherapy and hormone treatment. On completion there was a realisation that something was not as it should be: this turned into a 7 year journey, to uncover the truth and spread the word. Shirley's story starts as the treatment ends and the nightmare of the aftermath begins.

She is still living in France, Toulouse, and enjoying life in the beautiful Midi-Pyrenees.

Thank you for reading my 'memoir'.
I hope you have enjoyed this 'slice of my life' and I would love it if you could take the time to leave a review for my book on Amazon. Thank you so much.

I can be contacted on the following:

www.saledlie.com

email shirleyledlie@hotmail.com

twitter @SALedlie

Printed in Great Britain
by Amazon